Palgrave Studies of Entrepreneurship and Social Challenges in Developing Economies

Series Editor
Rajagopal, EGADE Business School, Tecnológico de Monterrey, Mexico City, Mexico

This series explores the role of entrepreneurship in managing social challenges comprising poverty, gender inequality, sustainability and climate change, income disparity, social healthcare, community housing and homelessness, and clean food and water supplies across Asia, Africa, and Latin America.

Entrepreneurship in developing countries has an economic motivation and it is taken up as a survival occupation. The books in this series discuss various attributes of social enterprises, innovation, technology, and the role of leadership in meeting the recurring social challenges. The discussion on entrepreneurship in this book series is central to social entrepreneurship, family enterprises, entrepreneurial business models, disruptive innovation, consumer behavior, marketing-mix, branding, profit and performance, market expansion, new product development, operations and supply chain, manufacturing, and servitization. In addition, the volumes in this book series also address the PESTEL (political, economic, social, technological, environmental, and legal) perspectives that support socio-economic development.

Rajagopal · Ananya Rajagopal

Unmasking Invisible Challenges in Entrepreneurship

Five Game Changer Models

palgrave
macmillan

Rajagopal
EGADE Business School
Tecnologico de Monterrey, Campus Santa Fe
Mexico, Mexico

Ananya Rajagopal
Universidad Anáhuac México
Mexico City, Mexico

ISSN 2731-6874 ISSN 2731-6882 (electronic)
Palgrave Studies of Entrepreneurship and Social Challenges in Developing Economies
ISBN 978-3-031-63652-3 ISBN 978-3-031-63653-0 (eBook)
https://doi.org/10.1007/978-3-031-63653-0

Cover illustration: Maram_shutterstock.com

This Palgrave Macmillan imprint is published by the registered company Springer Nature Switzerland AG
The registered company address is: Gewerbestrasse 11, 6330 Cham, Switzerland

With love to
Arati
Akhilesh, and
Niharika

Preface

In the changing scenario of accessible technology to micro, small, and medium enterprises, and developing their compatibility with industry 5.0, the technology-based enterprises are expected to play critical role in expanding existing markets by creating new consumption trends. The transcending technological innovation, and research and development have drawn the attention of governments in developing countries to provide large-scale financial support to local enterprises to improve market-oriented entrepreneurial skills. However, the support extended by the governmental and non-governmental organizations has yet to enhance their outreach to exhibit the desired impact on the economy of micro, small, and medium enterprises. It has been observed that in most developing countries, investment on research and development has failed to get the desired impact on technological innovation among the local enterprises.[1]

Local entrepreneurship has emerged as low-cost innovation for utilitarian products, which enables the masses not only to participate as potential customers, but also to serve as co-creators, suppliers, and producers. Therefore, local entrepreneurship focused on utilitarian products and inculcating social consciousness is considered as the key source

[1] Ahn, S., Kim, K.-S., and Lee, K.-H. (2022). Technological Capabilities, Entrepreneurship and Innovation of Technology-Based Start-Ups: The Resource-Based View. *Journal of Open Innovation: Technology, Market, and Complexity*, 8(3), 156–172.

of economic open innovation and business growth. These entrepreneurs are active social agents, who gather weight in crowdsourced innovations, social capital formation, and deriving business models from social networks.[2] Developing local area technology within the proximity of entrepreneurs and social ecosystem is one of the emerging challenges to provide cost-effective entrepreneurial growth. Innovation in local enterprises largely depends on the transfer of technology leading to business transformation and overall economic growth of enterprises.[3]

Entrepreneurship Change Agents

Evolving utilitarian technology markets in local enterprises not only offer a cost-effective market proposition, but also attract a great deal of attention as the new product innovations often create market continuum for utilitarian products. This requires a dynamic and skill-sensitive technology transfer environment to encourage entrepreneurs to continue with adaptation of changing technology and market ecosystem. However, transformation of local enterprises through transfer of technology and ubiquitous development of entrepreneurship has emerged as the joint responsibility of industry and local government. The transfer of technology to women entrepreneurs can be effective in a 6A model comprising Awareness (technology information), Attributes (markets and consumers), Association (consortium), Acquisition (low-cost innovation and technology), Appraisal (design thinking and marketability), and Alignment (empowerment, accountability, and responsiveness). This book discusses five critical game changer models linking local area transfer of technology to revamp innovation for social entrepreneurship for growth and acceleration, social ubiquity, and global accessibility of markets to entrepreneurship in a digital interface. These game changer models include discussion on following models:

[2] Si, S., Yu, X., Wu, A., Chen, S., Chen, S., and Su Y. (2015). Entrepreneurship and poverty reduction: a case study of Yiwu China. *Asia Pacific Journal of Management*, 32 (1), 119–143.

[3] Fontana, R. (2007). Technical change, prices and communications technology: Insights from the Local Area Networking industry. *Technological Forecasting and Social Change*, 74 (3), 313–330.

- Local Area Technology and Innovation for Transformation and Ubiquitous Development of Entrepreneurship (LATITUDE—Model 1).
- Growth and Acceleration in Restructuring Accountable Gender Entrepreneurship (GARAGE—Model 2)
- Revamping Innovation for Social Entrepreneurship (RISE—Model 3)
- Social Ubiquity of Innovation and Technology in Entrepreneurship (SUIT-E—Model 4)
- Global Accessibility to Markets and Entrepreneurship in a Digital Interphase (GAME-DI—Model 5).

The social and economic transformation at the bottom of the pyramid is shifting rapidly with the changing social and industrial development led by advancement in technology, the changing PNS factors, and relationship between the society and firms. The enterprises at the bottom line are grounded on social and ethnic foundations and are facing challenges to compete with aggressive innovation technology and manufacturing.[4] Therefore, the concept of advancement of people's actions and responsive technologies is critical to entrepreneurial development by integrating research (challenge based), innovation (low cost and incremental), sustainability (green consumption), and entrepreneurship (micro, small, and medium enterprises) to create and enhance socio-economic values of entrepreneurship. The social ubiquity provides entrepreneurs the collective perceptions to help in them understand the voice of customers, identify critical-to-quality elements, and appropriately manage the quality function deployment in the innovation and technology-led entrepreneurial projects. The social consciousness and consensus encourage entrepreneurs to adapt to just do it and just feel right notions to implement them in practice.

[4] Molina, A. and Rajagopal (2023). Challenge-based learning, research, and innovation: leveraging industry, government, and society. Cham, Switzerland: Springer, A Palgrave Macmillan imprint.

Thematic Flow

This book is divided into five chapters across three sections comprising Genesis, the Game Changers, and the Entrepreneurial Transformation. Based on the core arguments discussed above, Chapter 1 discusses the genesis of change in the context of changing global trends within industry 5.0 and technology ecosystem. The attributes of industry 5.0 in the context of technology transfer for development of micro, small, and medium enterprises have been discussed in this chapter with focus on achieving market competitiveness. The current status of local enterprises within the niche marketspace has been discussed in the context of family business system and operational ecosystem comprising manufacturing processes, technology, and innovation. This chapter also discusses ways to enable transitional enterprises to evolve with a competitive market-place and rapidly changing hybrid entrepreneurial domains. In addition, discussion on innovation and technology, technology-intensive enterprises, and public policies is also central to their discussion in this chapter.[5] Systems thinking in entrepreneurship encourages continuous learning and skill development to match with changing preferences of consumers and market competition. Applying systems thinking within the social and stakeholder ecosystem offers applied learning to firms, which enables them to enhance social proximity and systematically break the chaotic information to synthesize crowd-based business model.[6]

Entwining into the above logical framework, Chapter 2 discusses the attributes and consequences of systems thinking on enhancing the efficiency of entrepreneurship within the social and economic challenges. The market consciousness, innovation perspective, and consumer value creation as the tools for social proximity and crowd-based business modeling have also been discussed in this chapter. Contextualizing entrepreneurship with society and business discussions in this chapter focuses on enhancing social proximity of micro, small, and medium enterprises to develop interaction with internal and external stakeholders. The

[5] A. Newman, H.H. Tse, G. Schwarz, I. Nielsen (2018). The effects of employees' creative self-efficacy on innovative behavior: The role of entrepreneurial leadership. *Journal of Business Resrearch*, 89, 1–9.

[6] A. Tittel, O. Terzidis (2020), Entrepreneurial competences revised: Developing a consolidated and categorized list of entrepreneurial competences. Entrepreneurship Education, 3(1), 1–35.

discussions argue that social proximity will help in developing crowd-based business model and carrying out open innovations. In addition, the MIC factors comprising market consciousness, innovation perspectives, and creating consumer value have been discussed in this chapter. Discussion on advances in digital technologies, which have increased the possibilities of open innovation and outsourcing entrepreneurial activities to explore new opportunities, has also added value to this chapter.[7]

As the game changer models constitute the core of discussion of this book, Chapter 3 discusses the prelude to these models through the convergence of divergent factors of the game analytics. The PNS factors, increasing crowd influence, and socio-economic factors have been discussed in the book as the game foundation, which broadly deliberates R3 analytics comprising entrepreneurial attributes on resilience, returns, and risks. The transformational elements comprising technology, market, human elements, and organizational attributes in the context of local and global entrepreneurial environment have been discussed in this chapter. This chapter has comprehensively discussed the entrepreneurial transformation as a foundational attribute, which contributes to critical success of the firm and ensures long-term competitive success. The discussions also explore the role of government in supporting entrepreneurial transformation by resolving the visible and invisible challenges embedded in local firms[8] (*e.g.*, Liu & Lee, 2019). The crowd-based ideation, entrepreneurial blueprint, conceptualization, and decision making are critically examined in this chapter, which leads to discussion of ground-breaking concepts on the three-dimensional organizational square comprising organizational design, decision making, change management, and strategies and tactics.

Chapter 4 exhibits 'the game map' plotting five game changer models comprising local area technology and innovation for transformation and ubiquitous development of entrepreneurship (LATITUDE), growth and acceleration in restructuring accountable gender entrepreneurship (GARAGE), and revamping innovation for social entrepreneurship (RISE). Other two game changer models identified as social ubiquity of innovation and technology in entrepreneurship (SUIT-E) and

[7] Täuscher, K. (2017). Leveraging collective intelligence: How to design and manage crowd-based business models. *Business Horizons*, 60(2), 237–245.

[8] Liu, S. C.-H. and Lee, T. (2019). The multilevel effects of transformational leadership on entrepreneurial orientation and service innovation. *International Journal of Hospitality Management*, 82, 278–286.

global accessibility to markets and entrepreneurship in a digital interphase (GAME-DI) are also discussed as critical game changers contributing to the transformation of conventional entrepreneurship to technology-driven and market-oriented entrepreneurial business model. These game changer models have been evaluated from the perspective of value propositions, collective intelligence, extent of business transformation, environmental mining, and latent opportunities and threat. The above game changer models are significant in entrepreneurial development as a critical component of social and economic evolution in the current innovation and technology ecosystems. The importance of the proposed models has the potential to spark interest of government in developing economies to design compatible public programs to improve capability and competency of local enterprises[9] (*e.g.*, Pérez-Pérez et al., 2021).

Drawing the synergy from the previous chapters across two modules comprising The Genesis (Chapters 1 and 2) and The Game Changers (Chapters 3 and 4), the synthesis on entrepreneurial transformation has been discussed in Chapter 5 by convergence of divergent transformational factors and the philosophy of knowing-doing-being. The transcending innovation and technology, and rapidly changing market behavior requires entrepreneurial alignment through effective transformation. In this process, the resource-based enterprises stay ahead of large number of micro, small, and medium enterprises due to their limited resources and managerial capabilities. Based on the discussions on game changer models, game analytics, and their contextual relationship with entrepreneurship, this chapter deliberates ways to synchronize the entrepreneurial transitional pace. Accordingly, the transformational synergy across innovation, technology, market, and entrepreneurial growth has been discussed by converging the divergent transformational factors. In addition, the contributions of changing public policies and political ideologies to transformational entrepreneurship in developing economies also constitute the core discussion in this chapter. Future perspective on entrepreneurial transformation in the context of technology transfer, collective intelligence, and hybrid enterprises have also been discussed in this chapter.

[9] Pérez-Pérez, C., González-Torres, T., and Nájera-Sánchez, J.-J. (2021). Boosting entrepreneurial intention of university students: Is a serious business game the key?. *The International Journal of Management Education*, 19(3), https://doi.org/10.1016/j.ijme.2021.100506.

Mapping the Values

At the onset, this book discusses the genesis of change in local entrepreneurship, which has been acquired from transforming global trends and the impact of industry 5.0 on digitization of entrepreneurial firms to increase market competitiveness. The advancement of information and communication technology penetrated through the social media channels has significantly activated crowd cognition and collective intelligence as a radical game changer in local enterprises. The book argues that crowd-based entrepreneurial business models have encouraged E3 factors in entrepreneurship embedding people's engagement, empowerment of local entrepreneurs including gender sensitivity, and entrepreneurial performance with experience (learn and acquired skills). Further discussion in the book carries a thematic path by contextualizing socio-psychological and anthropological drivers in designing, developing, and delivering entrepreneurial business models within competitive market ecosystems.

The book also discusses the shortening of entrepreneurial proximity in competitive markets, which results in changing the entrepreneurial desire to foster new consumption patterns. The book argues that technology and new business models make the proximity proposition of local enterprises easier to move between consumers, alliance partners, and social institutions to improve the intertwining of consumption with low-cost innovation and marketing process. The game analytics in unmasking the challenges in transitional entrepreneurship has been discussed in the context of PNS factors. In addition, crowd influence towards ideation, design thinking, crowd funding, and brand-elevated marketing constitutes the core discussion in the book. R3 analytics discusses the social and entrepreneurial resilience to changing entrepreneurship style and argues the divergent factors of returns and risks to transitional and transformational entrepreneurship patterns. Based on these game analytics, a game map has been constructed with five entrepreneurial models as discussed in the pre-text.

Transformational entrepreneurship is a less explored area in the existing literature, though there is a plethora of studies on digitization of entrepreneurship and hybrid business models. However, the game changers such as crowd, social proximity, and virtual entrepreneurship have yet to be brought on to the surface. This book discusses the impact of public policies on entrepreneurial growth and prosperity in the context of global markets, reverse innovation, talent management at the grassroots, and capital integration strategies. Public policies have encouraged a single window system in developing countries to provide integrated resource support (capital, raw material, technology, and entrepreneurial skills) to entrepreneurial ventures. Public policies in Southeast Asia have helped emerging enterprises in rural and semi-urban areas to develop a systematic blueprint of technology integration and encourage hybrid entrepreneurial operations. The entrepreneurial education and skill development also constitute the core of public policies to drive faster and simplified growth pattern.

This book provides a different knowledge-scape to the readers in unveiling the iceberg challenges and offering solutions through five game changer entrepreneurial models covering wider geo-demographic landscape. This book converges the divergent factors of entrepreneurship with social and economic proximity to explore possibilities of business growth and entrepreneurial continuum. The discussions are supported by theoretical analysis, model blueprints, concept maps, and strategies for implementation of the suggested entrepreneurial models, which defines the unique knowledge diffusion framework of this book. This book summarizes effectively the attributes of changing entrepreneurial models and exploiting unique opportunities in competitive markets through advanced technologies at the grassroots. The book argues that identifying and scaling frugal, ambidextrous, and reverse innovation are critical to local entrepreneurship due to resources, technology, and skill development problems.

The Audience

The principal audience of this book are potential researchers interested in carrying out research based on entrepreneurial practices and their contributions to organizational design and operational efficiency in sustainable enterprises. This book helps to establish new research dimensions on convergence of entrepreneurial practices and dimensions of organizational development in emerging markets. This book also serves as a reference for the students of graduate management program studying in entrepreneurship stream, for learning the green entrepreneurial management patterns in emerging markets as suggested under sustainable development goals.

We hope this book will contribute to the existing literature and deliver new concepts to the students and researchers to pursue the subject further. By reading this book, policymakers, non-governmental organizations, and entrepreneurship development agencies will develop insights on how to converge innovation, technology, and business practices under changing entrepreneurial conditions.

Mexico City, Mexico
April 2024

Rajagopal
Ananya Rajagopal

Acknowledgments

Entrepreneurship and enterprise development have been the contemporary topics which have triggered a potential marketing approach to be explored while Professor Rajagopal was teaching courses on E-commerce Management, and Innovation and Global Competitiveness at Boston University. Proximity marketing has emerged as a promising decision-making domain in the information technology-based strategy platforms of firms. The core engagement of Professor Rajagopal in organizing first-in-series, the International Symposium on Entrepreneurship and Technology (SET-I) at metropolitan College, Boston University, during December 2023, has induced new insights in developing socio-economic and technology models to improve the entrepreneurship in developing countries. Such impetus has evolved discussion on game changer models in this book. Professor Rajagopal sincerely thanks Dr Tanya Zlateva, Dean, Metropolitan College of Boston University, for giving the opportunity to teach related subjects, which enabled him to meticulously develop and apply the research-based learning on technology-led entrepreneurship and business modeling in the classes. Discussions with Dr Vladimir Zlatev, Associate Professor of Practice at Administrative Sciences Department, Metropolitan College, Boston University, have also benefitted the horizon of knowledge on the subject immensely. Discussions with Dr Irena Vodenska, Department Chair, and Dr Marcus Goncalves, Associate Chair of the Department, on this topic also enriched the contents of this book.

Professor Rajagopal would like to acknowledge the support of Dr. Horacio Arredondo, Dean, EGADE Business School, and Dr Claudia Quintanilla, Director, Marketing and Business Intelligence Department of EGADE Business School, who have always encouraged him to take up new challenges in teaching graduate courses, develop new insights, and contribute to the existing literature prolifically. Professor Rajagopal thank all his students of graduate and doctoral programs at EGADE Business School for sharing enriching ideas on the subject during the classroom discussions, which helped in building this book on the framework of innovative ideas.

Ananya Rajagopal expresses sincere thanks to Jose Rodrigo Pozón López, Vice Rector (Academic), and Edgar González Olea, Dean of Business and Economics Division at Anahuac University, Mexico, for the encouragement to take up new research endeavors. She has been significantly educated by the comments and suggestions of various anonymous referees on her previous research works related to entrepreneurship, innovation, and marketing strategy that helped her in developing this contribution.

We express sincere thanks to Marcus Ballenger, Commissioning Editor, Scholarly Business, Palgrave Macmillan, for encouraging us to work on this research and accepting the proposal for publication. We are thankful to various anonymous referees of our previous research works on entrepreneurship, innovation, and technology management that helped us in looking deeper into the conceptual gaps and improving the quality with their valuable comments. Though it was a challenging journey with this publication project from ideation to manuscript preparation, we must acknowledge the encouragement from senior academics to proceed ahead with the project. We express our deep gratitude to Arati Rajagopal, who always reminded us of this task over other deadlines on the agenda. She also deserves kudos for copy editing the manuscript rigorously before submitting it to the publisher.

Contents

About the Authors

Rajagopal is Distinguished Professor of Marketing at EGADE Business School of Tecnologico de Monterrey (ITESM), at Mexico City Campus and Fellow of the Royal Society for Encouragement of Arts, Manufacture and Commerce, London. He is Fellow of the Chartered Management Institute and Fellow of Institute of Operations Management, UK. He is Visiting Professor at Boston University, Boston, Massachusetts, since 2013. He is also Visiting Professor since August 2020 at the UFV India Global Education of the University of the Fraser Valley, Canada, and teaches marketing-related courses. He has been listed with biography in various international directories.

He holds post-graduate and doctoral degrees in Economics and Marketing respectively from Pandit Ravishankar Shukla University in India. His specialization is in the field of Marketing Management. He has to his credit 75 books on marketing management and rural development themes, and over 400 research contributions that include published research papers in national and international refereed journals. He is Editor-in-Chief of International Journal of Leisure and Tourism Marketing and International Journal of Business Competition and Growth. He has been Associate Editor of Emerald Emerging Markets Case Studies (2012–2019), published by Emerald Publishers, UK. He is on the editorial board of various journals of international repute.

He has been conferred the honor of Distinguished Professor by the EGADE Business School, Mexico, in 2020. His research contributions have been recognized by the National Council of Science and Technology (CONACyT), Government of Mexico, by awarding him the highest level of National Researcher-SNI Level- III in 2013. He has been awarded UK-Mexico Visiting Chair 2016–2017 for collaborative research on 'Global-Local Innovation Convergence' with University of Sheffield, UK, instituted by the Consortium of Higher Education Institutes of Mexico and UK. He has been conferred the Overseas Indian Award (*Pravasi Bhartiya Samman Award*) in January 2023 for his outstanding contribution in the field of Education. This is the highest honor conferred by the President of India. This award has been conferred in acknowledgment of the outstanding achievement in the field of Education in India, USA, and Mexico.

Ananya Rajagopal obtained PhD degree in Administration with focus on Entrepreneurship and Marketing Strategies from EGADE Business School, Tecnológico de Monterrey. She obtained her Master of Business Administration (MBA) degree from Alliant International University, San Diego, specializing in Strategic Management. She has obtained two Bachelor of Science degrees: B.S. Industrial and Systems Engineering from the Tecnológico de Monterrey, and BS in International Business Administration from Alliant International University, San Diego. She has ample experience in the financial industry in Mexico City since 2006.

She has published several papers in international journals of repute and contributed research works in international conferences and edited books. She is author of the four books comprising Managing Startup Enterprises in Emerging Markets: Leadership Dynamics and Marketing Strategies, Epistemological Attributions to Entrepreneurial Firms: Linking Organizational Design and Operational Efficiency, Women Entrepreneurs in Emerging Markets: Managing Performance within Ecosystems, and Towards Cleaner Entrepreneurship: Bridging Social Consciousness and Sustainability. She is reviewer of several journals of international repute including Emerald Emerging Markets Case Studies, Journal of Transnational Management, and Journal of Strategy and Management. She is also a member advisory panel of Elsevier Insights. She has presented her research in the high-order professional international bodies including Academy of Management, Academy of Marketing Science, and Association for Consumer Research. She currently holds a position of Research Professor at Universidad Anáhuac Mexico.

List of Figures

PART I

At the Grassroots

CHAPTER 1

The Genesis

Abstract This chapter discusses the genesis of change in the context of changing global trends within industry 5.0 and technology ecosystem. There are innovative ways to enable transitional enterprises to evolve with competitive marketplace and rapidly changing hybrid entrepreneurial domains. In addition, discussion on innovation and technology, technology-intensive enterprises, and public policies is also central to their discussion in this chapter. The discussion in this chapter also includes the role of systems thinking in continuous learning and skill development of entrepreneurs to match with changing preferences of consumers and market competition. Applying systems thinking within the social and stakeholder ecosystem offers applied learning to firms. Systems thinking enhances social proximity and systematically break the chaotic information to synthesize crowd-based business model, which constitute the core discussions in this chapter.

Keywords Innovation and technology · Industry 5.0 · Market competitiveness · Niche marketing · Entrepreneurial domains · Family business

Rajagopal and A. Rajagopal, *Unmasking Invisible Challenges in Entrepreneurship*, Palgrave Studies of Entrepreneurship and Social Challenges in Developing Economies,
https://doi.org/10.1007/978-3-031-63653-0_1

Entrepreneurship is experienced today as a commercial venture beyond the conventional philosophies of subsistence and family-oriented occupation. Commercialization of entrepreneurship in the growing innovation and technology ecosystems embodies social, cultural, economic, ethnic, and anthropological perspectives by putting the market first. Accordingly, transition in the entrepreneurial trends is largely affected by the consumer preferences, market trends, underlying innovations, and competitive strategies, which often act as entrepreneurial game changers affecting the commercial perspectives of entrepreneurship. In both developed and developing economies, start-ups have been synonymous to entrepreneurship and have evolved as family businesses by focusing on their home markets. However, entrepreneurial transition in the age of continuous innovation and technology has been considered as *born-global enterprise*, which focuses on exploring opportunities beyond territorial boundaries in a cyberspace. A technology-led entrepreneurship achieves competitiveness and profitability through continuous learning and developing new knowledge through research and development to explore new markets. They are instrumental not only in manufacturing innovative products, but also in expanding employment through consortiums and penetrating the existing markets to expand their business (Ahn et al., 2022).

Most enterprises today are built with information and communication technology by enhancing proximity and outreach to markets, learning to manage distant operations, and exploring the competitive advantages in manufacturing and marketing operations. The uniqueness of enterprises today is frugal innovations, challenging the latent demand, and overshadowing the existing product-market scenarios to unmask the new dimensions of products to attract customers. Innovative enterprises tend to polarize customers towards their innovative products and services through disruptive strategies to develop a unique niche (Bosco et al., 2019). The major challenge for the upcoming micro enterprises is to develop congruence with social values and influence the local markets to attract utilitarian innovation as the key change agents for socio-economic growth continuum. However, to get along with market trends, individual entrepreneurship is gradually transforming into entrepreneurial guilds and consortiums under the shared-economy principles to reduce risk, increase entrepreneurial returns, and ensure recovery through collective operations (Ratten & Jones, 2021). Consortium entrepreneurship has emerged as a market enabler by streamlining the technology-led supply chain manufacturing and marketing strategies. Consequently, entrepreneurship today is built around integrated resource theory by combining capital, technology, and managerial know-how to achieve strategic entrepreneurship goals. With the growing technological capabilities, entrepreneurship is driven by both human capital and knowledge capital, which enhances entrepreneurial competence, leadership, and design thinking for continuous innovations (Seungku et al., 2022). These factors affect the way entrepreneurs develop and implement ideas to structure their business plan and drive significant impact on their performance in competitive marketplace (Zahra, 2021).

Innovations blended with artificial intelligence and machine learning drive enterprises to develop technology-led utilitarian products and create market demand for manufactured products with long-term perceived use values. Therefore, successful introduction of new products by transitional enterprises is often not-streamlined, as each innovation requires a new path to market. Though innovation contributes significantly to the competitive advantage, the consumers' preference to brand and inculcated perceived use value makes a greater difference in creating market demand, sales growth, and competitive advantage (Giasolli et al., 2021). The industry attractiveness in the context of transcending competition and underlying substitution effect influences the innovation and technology. Therefore, the broad characteristics of entrepreneurial firms today include the attributes such as product diversification, research and development of capabilities, and product-market fit beyond the size of the firms. The entrepreneurial competition is continuously growing in rapidly changing marketplace due to transitions in consumer preferences (Salamzadeh et al., 2022). Consequently, the entrepreneurial knowledge on technology development based on innovation count, innovation process, and market indicators affects the entrepreneurial performance. The economic value of entrepreneurship driven by disruptive innovations tends to be heterogeneous and difficult to streamline with the goals of large industries. Most micro and small enterprises are highly active in developing innovative products but fail to protect their intellectual property by patenting them. Consequently, most entrepreneurial innovations are acquired by large firms without formal terms of reference and convert such entrepreneurial innovations into reverse innovations (Leyden & Link, 2015).

Industry 5.0

Advancement in information and communication technology (ICT) has encouraged entrepreneurial firms to shift their business processes to digital platforms breaking down industry barriers and creating new opportunities overriding the conventional business models. In this process, the resistance to change has increased as their long, successful, and conventional business models have been compromised by digital disruptions (Camisón-Haba et al., 2019). However, as a contemporary option to gain business competitiveness, firms need to accept the transitional threats and explore opportunities in creating new generation businesses, which are more connected to futuristic digital ecosystem. The revolution in industrial growth has witnessed various stages of transition, which influences the manufacturing and operations processes with the fast-moving technological intervention. The industry 4.0 is transiting today from automation and digitization of processes to industry 5.0, which combines the human factor with machine learning to customize manufacturing, operations, and marketing practices (Carayannis et al., 2021). The new stage of industrial revolution combines human skills with artificial intelligence (AI) and machine learning (ML) to improve the efficiency and accuracy of mechanical output controlled by robotics. Emerging enterprises of various sizes across the cyber-physical space in global ecosystem are relying on AI and ML by improving the human abilities in computer-aided creativity, decision making, and solving complex problems. The industry 5.0 accordingly sets a new trend in business by encouraging highly personalized and demand-led manufacturing through AI and ML advantages (Wang et al., 2016). These technologies converge collaborative robotics, exoskeleton, and augmented reality (AR) within sophisticated AI systems. The emerging firms today use virtual reality (VR), augmented reality, and metaverse reality (MR) to establish closer interaction between human element and machine-led business. It is the right time for the firms to evaluate the threats and opportunities in the technology transitions and create appropriate business models to connect with advanced digital ecosystem (Xu et al., 2021). Service enterprises like Air BnB, Uber, and Amazon are gradually driving transition of their services to leverage customer relationship and reduce the cost-time-risk (CTR) factors. The major challenge in such transition process is to integrate value chains of conventional systems with the new technology ecosystem and develop distinctive business models by enhancing the capabilities, competencies, and business relationships. The industry 5.0 is the fifth industrial revolution, which is largely driven by the AI, ML, and large language modeling (LLM). The transcending growth of information and communication technology and its easy accessibility among local enterprises has significantly boosted the use of technology applications and platforms by micro, small, and medium enterprises in product designing, manufacturing, supply chain management, marketing, and managing customer relations. The accessibility to the information and communication technology has been widely supported by the public policies, non-governmental organizations, and entrepreneurial guilds within the community growth models in developing economies. Such human-technology interface at community level within the entrepreneurial ecosystem of developing economies helps in converging the operations of micro, small, and medium enterprises with the attributes of industry 5.0 revolution, which is penetrating geo-demographic segments ambidextrously.

Convergence of local enterprises with industry 5.0 attributes is gradually increasing but not to the scale of business. Most micro, small, and medium enterprises evolve from family businesses and grow with centralized leadership acquired through succession in the family, which narrows down the prospects of community orientation within the social domain as exhibited in Table 1.1. The incumbents in family businesses opt for intra-family succession and not to hand-over the business to parties outside the family including employees or other businesses, which limits the possibilities of mergers and acquisitions (Symeonidou et al., 2022). Consequently, entrepreneurial practices are largely driven by conventional wisdom, which often stand resilient to change. The centralized leadership often affects the stakeholder engagement in creativity and decision making as micro, small, and medium enterprises are the outgrowth of family business; the gender participation and work-life balance have been challenging alongside the perspectives of inclusivity and diversity in enterprise. One of the critical success factors of micro, small, and medium enterprises is to align with industry 5.0 attributes by developing sustainability in manufacturing and supply chain management, and in developing workplace agility. The industry 5.0 with focus on virtual enterprise operations tends to create social value and community welfare through human-centric approach. The convergence of conventional practices with virtual competence in industry 5.0 helps in managing high-value tasks by developing compatibility with PNS factors within the lean work environment.

Table 1.1 Convergence of local entrepreneurship with industry 5.0 Attributes

Domains	*Entrepreneurial ecosystem*	*Conventional practices*	*Industry 5.0 attributes*	*Convergence and growth perspectives*
Social	Family business Leadership succession Community orientation	Resilience to change Stakeholder engagement Work-life balance Inclusivity and diversity	Social value Community welfare Workplace agility Sustainability	Human-centric approach PNS compatibility High-value tasks Lean work environment
Economic	Resource-based view Resource utilization Profit perspectives	Resources limitation Resources efficiency Cost and risk creep CTR effects	Low cost high value Network effects Input–output efficiency Programmability	Projection-based investment High economic returns CTR balance
Innovation	Sluggish Innovation Fear of failure Attributes of risk	Niche-based innovation Marginalization effects Conventional wisdom Returns on innovation	Project-based learning Crowdsourcing Collective intelligence AI-led innovation Business-linked innovation	AI design thinking Need-based innovation Innovation proximity and profitability Continuous improvement V-H innovation space
Technology	Experiential knowledge Community acceptance Entrepreneurial capabilities	Technology adaptation Perceived use value Ease of use Life cycle and risk factors	Transformational view Viability and feasibility Regenerative value Virtual leap Digital trends and metaverse	Economic growth High production and consumption Equitable prosperity Multi-tasking with agility Lean principles

(continued)

Table 1.1 (continued)

Domains	*Entrepreneurial ecosystem*	*Conventional practices*	*Industry 5.0 attributes*	*Convergence and growth perspectives*
Business and Operations	Niche business model Low-cost low-risk maxim Subsistence business Low value chain	Low engagement Low investment Centralized decision making Defensive business	Digital technologies Competitiveness Market-linked solutions Sustainable operations Data analytics Flexible business process	Hyper connectivity Data centricity Risk mitigation Profit orientation Simulation and synergy Social alignment Physical and virtual spaces

Source Authors

The economic domain of entrepreneurial ecosystem at the grassroots largely manages through resource-based view with limited profit perspectives due to the challenges in resource utilization. Such entrepreneurial conditions emerge due to resource limitations (capital, human, and technological resources) causing low efficiency in resources utilization. The unplanned investments to improve productions and operations efficiencies in these enterprises result into cost and risk creep, which adversely affect the cost, time, and risk appropriations (Tomizawa et al., 2020). Therefore, aligning with industry 5.0 attributes helps these enterprises to achieve input–output efficiency, programmability in manufacturing, and supply chain management. In addition, these enterprises are benefitted from the adaptation to information and communication technology platforms, which provide pro-business network effects leading to low-cost and high-value restoration in enterprises. The virtual alignment in micro, small, and medium enterprises helps in achieving CTR balance to generate high economic returns and ensure projection-based investment (forecast).

Commonly, innovations in micro, small, and medium enterprises tend to be sluggish due to the financial attributes of risk and fear of failure. These factors lead to low-cost niche-based vertical innovations, which marginalize the returns on innovation and marginalize the performance (Koo & Eesley, 2021). The niche-based innovations are largely based on conventional wisdom, and they marginally support the profitability goals.

The industry 5.0 encourages continuous innovation through project-based learning and crowdsourcing to identify the innovation goals based on PNS factors. The AI-led innovation is streamlined with appropriate business linkages to ensure returns on investment. The combination of collective intelligence and AI helps in design thinking process to invest in need-based innovation process and enhance the proximity of innovation to create value and profitability (Wurth et al., 2021). The alignment of niche-based innovations of micro, small, and medium enterprises with AI-led innovations under industry 5.0 ecosystem helps enterprises to develop vertical and horizontal (V-H) innovation space to create value, business performance, and desired profit (Pustovrh et al., 2020).

The enterprises at the grassroots commonly refrain from using high-value technology due to low capabilities and competencies. These enterprises are largely based on experiential knowledge, community acceptance, and stay risk averse from adapting to new technologies despite several pro-profit endorsements of such technologies. However, the pertinent question in adapting to technologies in micro, small, and medium enterprises is about the lifecycle of technology and the associated risk factors. Consequently, adaptation to technology is subjective to the perceived use value and ease of use of technology among entrepreneurs. Overcoming the conventional barriers on use of technology, the industry 5.0 with focus on AI, ML, and LLM offers transformational view of technology adaptation with economic viability and technological feasibility through digital trends and virtual leap in technology applications to regenerate the entrepreneurial value. In addition, digital trends in enterprise management such as metaverse lead to faster economic growth with high productivity and consumption economics. The adaptation to technology under industry 5.0 ecosystem, multi-tasking with agility following the lean principles provides higher economic and equitable prosperity. Accordingly, many entrepreneurs engaged in manufacturing and services have overcome the market niches and expanded their business targeting the multi-geo-demographic segments with revived entrepreneurial goals (Chaudhry et al., 2024).

The discussion on social, economic, innovation, and technology domains of entrepreneurial ecosystem explains the benefits in aligning with industry 5.0 attributes for economic growth perspectives. Streamlining these domains with industry 5.0 significantly affects the business and operations of micro, small, and medium enterprises to overcome the niche business model and low-cost low-risk maxim of subsistence business with low value chain. These conventional attributes demonstrate low engagement, low investment, centralized decision making, and implementing defensive strategies in business by these enterprises. However, the alignment with the industry 5.0 ecosystem revamps the entrepreneurial capabilities and competencies through digital technologies, which increases market competitiveness of these enterprises through market-linked solutions and sustainable operations. The data analytics and flexible business processes help in mitigating risk through data analytics, hyper connectivity with market players, and developing omnipresence with physical and virtual spaces as digital twins (Ouahabi et al., 2024).

Technology-based start-ups in the contemporary technological environment strive to acquire new knowledge, experiment new business models, and gain competitive advantage in new markets parallel to conventional niches. Such start-ups try to achieve breakeven in their business with intensive production and marketing within niche without spatial expansion of business. The intensive business models can be well executed to achieve market competitiveness using technology platforms combining AR and VR strategies within AI and ML technological environment. Large-scale financial support of the government in the developing economies towards converging small enterprises with industry 5.0 revolution has significantly supported these firms to adapt to technological innovations and improve technological capabilities and competencies (Leng et al., 2023). The regional technological development is highly skewed and varied due to socio-economic and behavioral challenges causing obstructions in diffusing technology-based knowledge, sharing innovation networks, and developing entrepreneurial capital. Consequently, there is a high growth of nascent enterprises in developing economies as compared to the technology-led high-growth firms commonly identified as *gazells*, which play significant role in driving regional entrepreneurship and economic growth (Acs & Mueller, 2007). However, high-growth entrepreneurship is seeking to fill the technology gap and develop an entrepreneurial ecosystem conducive to technology-led high-growth entrepreneurship in the industry 5.0 revolution. The high-growth entrepreneurship using technology platforms to develop advanced business models amplifies the CTR factors to transform existing businesses to gain competitive advantage (Audretsch et al., 2008).

Industry 5.0 sets priority to human centricity by aligning AI, ML, and robotics in managing productivity. Environmental, social, and governance (ESG) is increasingly being used to evaluate the performance of industry 5.0, which aims at converging technology with collective intelligence and in establishing network economics (Lee et al., 2022). There is an increasing realization in developing economies that industrial success combining with the advancement of information and communication technology will help in leveraging creative workplaces that are human centered within the social ecosystem. The differentiating feature of the industrial revolution 5.0 establishes economic and social balance through responsible governance by transiting the conventional processes to a digital society. This stage of industrial revolution conjoins the Schumpeterian philosophy, which argues that economic growth is driven by innovation and entrepreneurship with changing forms of technology, communication, and processes (Maddikunta et al., 2022). The evolution of industrial revolution has significantly supported entrepreneurial creativity, manufacturing, and transformative developments in all techno-economic subsystems of the society. The introduction of new social concepts such as sustainability, human centricity, and technology-driven production exhibits new challenges to identify PNS factors and develop need-based solutions under industry 5.0 workspace environment (Rajagopal, 2024). In addition, convergence of human-cyber-physical system has been integrated in multi-objective entrepreneurial task optimization to foster socio-economic development, sustainability, and industrial growth at the grassroots. Such synchronization of resources and processes results into fostering society, strategies, and sustainability to improve technology-industry collaboration (Zhou et al., 2019).

Most developing economies are engaged in connecting local enterprises with multinational corporations (MNCs) as feeder manufacturing channels by promoting consortium strategy and funding local enterprises at the grassroots to improve technology-oriented productivity. The global MNCs serve as the resource base to local enterprises and improve contextual manufacturing and marketing factors, which help global–local industrial tie-ups to improve omnipresence and develop hybrid competitive strategy. The industry 5.0 significantly supports the evolution of such symbiosis between global and local firms and motivates them to benefit from favorable cost structures and innovations across the business tiers (Gabrielsson et al., 2016). The technological intervention in micro, small, and medium enterprises has significantly contributed to improving the industrial presence of this sector by implementing the hybrid competitive strategies to enhance both industrial presence and social presence. The key resources in entrepreneurial advancement alongside the globalization have been supported under public policies towards funding and risk absorption. The inter- and intra-firm networks have significantly supported the design thinking, creativity, resource exchange, workspace sharing, ownership advantages, and diffusion of knowledge across different layers of industries (Eng & Ozdemir, 2014). The knowledge integration and inter-firm networks have strongly supported the grassroots level enterprises to stay competitive in high-technology markets and establish significant global synergies in marketing. Making cyber-physical space in the high-technology market has been the requirement for emerging enterprises to develop corporate competitiveness and technology-driven strategies to ensure performance by achieving differentiation and cost advantage (Hughes et al., 2010).

The factors contributing to convergence of the advancing information and communication technologies in transformation of grassroots enterprises are exhibited in Fig. 1.1. The synergy between industry 5.0 and technology entrepreneurship has driven new market order, which has established industry symbiosis between innovative start-ups and large corporations in manufacturing cost-effective innovative products with the potential of global branding and marketing to serve the changing consumer preferences. Technology thrust has been the core impetus in transforming family entrepreneurship by enhancing technology-led entrepreneurial competence to improve techno-economic contributions to industry and social values. The digital ecosystem is continuously changing due to advancement of technology and its intervention in business. The techno-economic subsystems have been significantly driven by the collaborative robotics between expert firms and start-ups to homogenize the use of technology and develop an appropriate triadic fit of technology-industry-market paradigm as illustrated in Fig. 1.1. The focus of industry 5.0 is to develop a technology and social balance through human centricity in using technology. The environmental and social governance has been a growing global concern in integrating technology with entrepreneurial development. The collective intelligence and knowledge management practices have significantly contributed to developing ICT and ESG practices.

The technology thrust through continuous advancement of ICT has promoted new technology dimensions of AI and ML, which resulted in changing the perspectives of business modeling using AR, VR, and MR platforms to develop business-consumer networks. Such advancements have significantly improved the business performance,

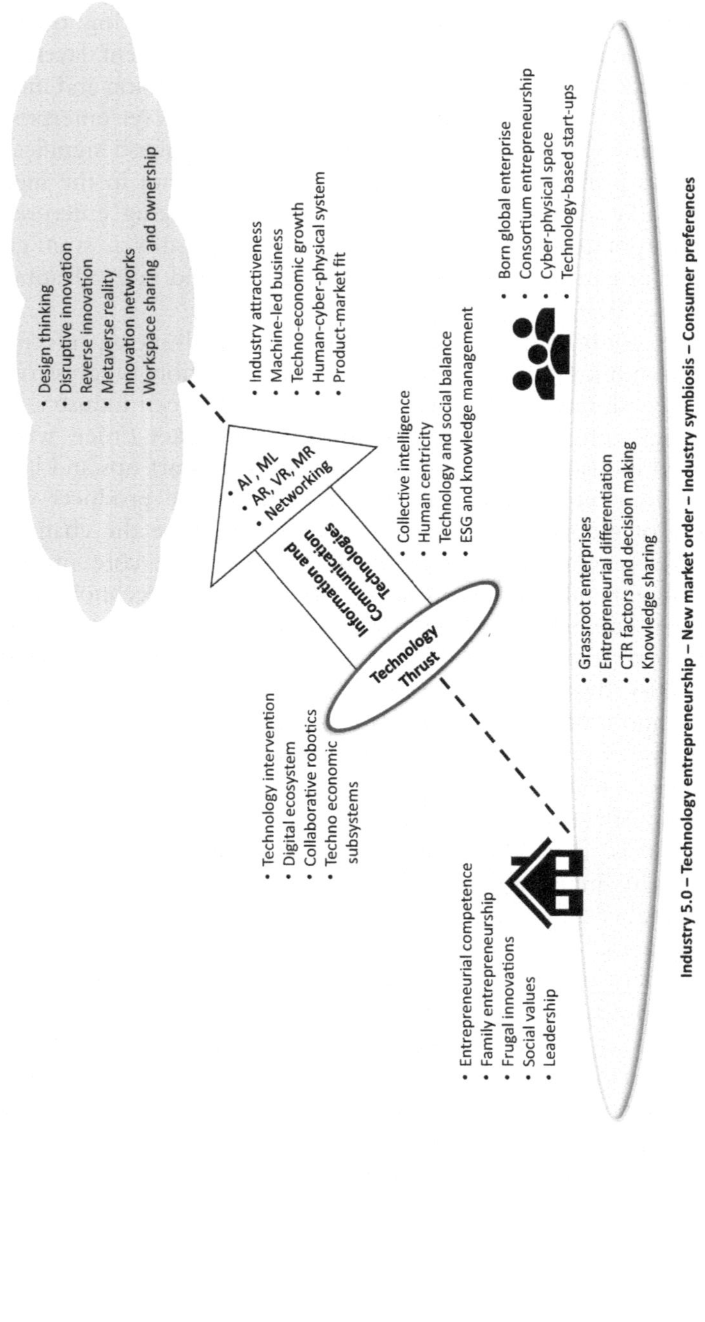

Fig. 1.1 Entrepreneurial elevation from ground to cloud (*Source* Authors)

consumer convenience, and market competitiveness. With the advancement of ICT, attractiveness between industry and market has been well established in the twenty-first century, which promoted techno-economic growth by integrating the human-cyber-physical systems. Such process integration has ensured product-market fit in the machine-led entrepreneurial ecosystem. The growing effects of technology intervention in entrepreneurship and marketing have enabled computer-aided design thinking, which has caused widespread disruptive innovation to drive away the conventional effects of entrepreneurship. The growing business concerns on developing symbiotic relationship between human-cyber-physical systems have motivated firms to build hybrid business models by sharing workspace and ownership to improve innovation networks and their positive effects. The contextual development in business using AI–ML technology sphere has witnessed metaverse reality as an outgrowth of technology-led business modeling. Figure 1.1 emphasizes on various attributes of *born-global* enterprise, which have grown with technology and connected to all layers of industries by size, operation, and spatial distribution. Consequently, the philosophy of consortium entrepreneurship linking small and large enterprises with various industrial operations has merged in the cyber-physical space. Over time, the consortium entrepreneurship has encouraged nascent industries to grow around technology, innovation, and cyber-physical markets. However, CTR factors have been the prime concern for enterprises of all sizes to make appropriate decisions to integrate technology in business and earmark entrepreneurial differentiation. The knowledge sharing through enterprise networking, leader-member exchange, and collective intelligence play critical role in deriving techno-economic benefits in both upstream and downstream markets.

Digital transformation strategies have become a major challenge for conventional small and medium enterprises as they differ in the motivation and target of transformation, leadership style, importance of skills like creativity and entrepreneurial spirit. These enterprises suffer from the fear of potential failure during the digital transformation process. In addition, employees are also intolerant to risks and challenges faced in the process and possess lack of managerial tactics to gain quick stability in business. By providing heuristics and a systematic basis for comparison of different strategies, it is believed that the proposed framework will be useful to researchers and managers responsible for and interested in digital transformation. Multinational companies have shown interest in acquiring the local enterprises by committing resources to fugal and reverse innovation initiatives such as training to accelerate the growth of start-ups, which was supported by the Microsoft Corporation in India. In addition, large companies are engaged in eliminating the conventional systems by introducing gradual transformation. The conventional work process of small enterprises constrains the productivity, cost, time, and quality and involves risks in working with large companies (Prashantham & Yip, 2016). Digital marketing has opened massive opportunities to deliver new consumer experiences and strengthened the relationships with consumers across destinations in the global marketplace. Digital disruption has created new dimensions in consumer marketing to drive compulsive buying behavior through the benefits of large-scale promotions and convenience. Platform economy has shown a huge shift in creation of consumer value. The platform economy distinctly comprises a new set of business and economic relations that depend on the Internet, computation, and data (Rajagopal, 2021a, 2021b). Consequently, the industrial revolution adapted to the technological progress and began to keep pace with the population. Such growth in the industrial products and services for consumption and business needs created new markets, and the global transformation in product and financial markets was observed by the middle of the nineteenth century. The customer-centric marketing approaches gave an easy access to the multinational companies to develop latitudinal expansion of their business and penetrate the local markets. Accordingly, relationships with customers and global–local alliances have grown as critical success factors for multinational companies engaged in marketing. The increased interest in these concepts has triggered a paradigm shift from mass marketing towards relationship marketing. It has been observed by the end of twentieth century that only a relationship orientation secures firms' success (Hedaa & Ritter, 2005). The theories of social identity, persuasion, and multiculturalism have motivated global–local moves among the multinational companies to do business in the local geo-demographic market segments. Ethnic marketing has the potential to reach the diverse consumer segments across regions and generational cohorts. Ethnicity attributes in marketing have driven the local enterprises to develop tie-up alliances with multinational firms. Ethnic marketing approaches develop a strong socio-cultural sensitivity that bridges the global–local differences in geo-demographic expansion of companies (Harrison et al., 2017; Licsandru & Cui, 2019; Rajagopal, 2020).

Market Competitiveness

In the growing technology-driven product-market mix and the market competition today, most companies focus on expanding their market by synchronizing cyber-physical market space. The global market competitiveness has been influenced by the technology intervention, which has significantly affected the business models of the firms and consumer behavior. As consumers are the pivot of business, the power of innovation and technology has significantly driven the market attractiveness and consumer psychodynamics. Such transformation in the marketplace has driven consumers towards making competitive buying decisions. Technology-led enterprises often present disruptive marketing solutions to gain competitive advantage by providing an array of innovations and a new consumption space to drive acquisition of consumers and retain them as technology loyal. Therefore, a company in a competitive marketplace must manage customers by catering to their preferences and values, and exhibiting how products or services can help solve each buyer's problems. Consumers today are highly influenced by the fast-growing technologies, which enable them to adapt to convenience consumption practices. It makes them stand by changing technologies and innovations to derive relative advantages and satisfaction in consumption. Consequently, the consumer philosophy of touch-feel-pick has significantly altered their behavior towards consumption of utilitarian products. Accordingly, they do not buy products; instead, they buy solutions, which endorses the importance of PNS factors in developing market competitiveness for the firms. Such transformation in firms and consumption behavior sets atop the technology in business modeling and in developing marketing strategies. It is a must for managers to learn to reap the enormous benefits of loyalty by developing technology-driven relationships with consumers to guide them in making a right decision in marketing. To achieve these ends, firms should be able to understand the dynamics of consumer behavior and derive benefits from behavioral analytics in making appropriate marketing decisions. Start-up enterprises with innovative products and services must integrate PNS factors in developing innovative products to achieve market competitiveness through social networks of marketing. Such technology-driven competitiveness encourages the expansion of business in future and builds market competitiveness by co-creating values and co-evolving design thinking process to enhance customer value and competitive advantages (Rajagopal, 2019).

Market competitiveness is affected by the elements of industry attractiveness comprising the growth of competing enterprises and the derived substitution effect of identical and similar products in the marketplace. It is common to expect high growth of competing enterprises operating on the low CTR factors within niche markets. The innovative products of start-up enterprises often succumb to such identical competition as they fail to establish product differentiation and create customer value. The products of such enterprises are less competitive due to high bargaining power of consumers and suppliers within the industry. In addition, the dynamics of market competition is also governed by the speed of new entrants and consistency in marketing of parallel products (Rajagopal, 2019). Consequently, profit potential of a market is determined by the industry attractiveness in reference to the speed of new companies entering the industry, and availability of substitute products. The product differentiation is determined by the convergence of innovation and technology with CTR factors to establish brand loyalty and override the product substitution effects. In addition, the bargaining power of consumers and suppliers also governs the competitiveness of the companies within the industry. The magnitude and the direction of market share and profitability for the companies within the industry help enterprises to determine the market competitiveness of brands (Tong Qin & Liu, 2019). The enterprise scaling in the context of existing market competition is judgmental for the firms in the niche markets to determine their market competitiveness and relative profitability. Therefore, enterprises can increase their competitiveness in the market by creating brand equity, trust, loyalty, and differentiation between other competitive offerings in the market (Veloutsou et al., 2020).

The rapid growth in technology and innovation of new products is changing the scenario of consumer products industry, as competition is becoming dynamic, altering the industry attractiveness frequently. The industry 5.0 has increased technology and market competitiveness through intelligent manufacturing (AI and ML based) and innovations across different sizes of enterprises. The technology competitiveness has become the corner stone of affordable innovation and market competitiveness by combining high productivity, quality, and adaptability at minimum cost. Accordingly, large effects have been found in manufacturing, marketing, and business growth, which contributed significantly to the development of local markets besides globalization drive. Technology, innovation, and market competition have become increasingly intensive over time (Wu et al., 2022). The unpredictability in many industries like consumer electronics, automobiles, food and beverages, and fashion industry is continuously increasing due to short innovation and technology life cycles. The attractiveness in the automobile industry is changing fast in view of the new technology disruptions. With the advancement of ICT, various forms of competition in the market have engrossed the business growth of firms at various geo-demographic levels, which are experienced in business-to-business, business-to-consumers, consumer-to-consumer (network marketing), and online-to-offline (hybrid marketing). The competition is increasing across the above taxonomy of marketing by determining the new order of global markets, diffusion of information and communication technologies, and decentralized marketing network. Due to the entropy in marketing taxonomy, multi-channel practices, creation of customer values in fragmented subdomains, and integrating the transfer of knowledge in achieving market competitiveness are becoming increasingly challenging (Gabrielsson et al., 2016). Technological readiness, innovative players, and start-ups contribute an important dimension in the development of autonomous vehicles over the hybrid and electric categories.

Regulation and consumer acceptance represent additional dynamics for autonomous vehicles. Such market scenario in the automobile industry has strengthened the bargaining power of consumers and distributors. Many new players are likely to enter the market, especially resource-rich high-tech companies and start-ups in the emerging markets. These new entrants from outside the industry are also wielding more influence with consumers and regulators. However, once these challenges are addressed in the industry, autonomous vehicles will offer tremendous value for consumers (Gao et al., 2016). In view of increasing congestion of the firms with identical objective of enhancing market share through the cost and price leadership, developing competitive marketing strategies requires high differentiation by applying the hybrid strategies to ensure differentiated value creation. The high-technology markets promise higher growth in business through continuous innovation; however, firms need to guard against uncertainty and dynamism of consumer preferences. Therefore, firms must develop strategies considering VRINE aspects, which consist of value, rarity, inimitability, non-substitutability, and exploitability of market demand and consumer preferences. It has been argued that specific organizational structure with inclusivity and diversity encourages enterprises to gain competitive advantage from differentiated strategy and streamlined enterprise consumer knowledge transfers (Tsai & Hsu, 2014). The degree of rivalry among different firms is a function of the number of competitors, industry growth, asset intensity, product differentiation, and exit barriers. Among these, the most influential variables are identified as the number of competitors and industry growth. Industries with high fixed costs tend to be more competitive because competing firms cut price to be able to operate at the economies of scale. However, with the differentiation strategy, the rivalry within industry is reduced among the products and services offered by the competitors, in both real and perceived senses. Another significant concept associated with the industry attractiveness and competitiveness is the difficulty of exit from an industry due to the damage of brand risk and corporate image (Rajagopal, 2022).

The advancement in manufacturing technology and innovation with the engagement of ICT and cloud business environment has inculcated a behavioral push among micro, small, and medium enterprises to open their niche market and drive through the transitional market applying technology-led operational strategies. Figure 1.2 illustrates the dynamics of market transition and competitiveness explaining the attributes of market taxonomy comprising niche market, transitional market, and contemporary market. The basic principle of niche market as minimum viable segment tends to shift to new paradigm of marketing led by the developments in ICT, AI, and ML. The niche markets focusing on minimum viable segments have been using low-cost technology, which have shown resistance to adapt to advanced technologies due to CTR limitations. Consequently, micro, small, and medium enterprises are trailing behind to explore cyber-physical market space. The conventional manufacturing process in these enterprises often raises ambiguity in cost-price-quality relationship causing low brand loyalty and high consumer defection. Therefore, enterprises that can absorb risk are influenced by the output of new technology adaptation using advanced features of ICT, AI, and ML factors to develop congruence with the changing consumer preferences. Accordingly, most enterprises are transiting from the niche market by establishing their products and services as disruptive innovations in transitional markets.

Entrepreneurs face many operational challenges while transiting from the niche markets and conventional marketing practices, which causes streamlining the design-to-market strategies. Micro, small, and medium enterprises often face VRINE risk factors, which are experienced in consumer value creation, highlighting differentiators to create rarity

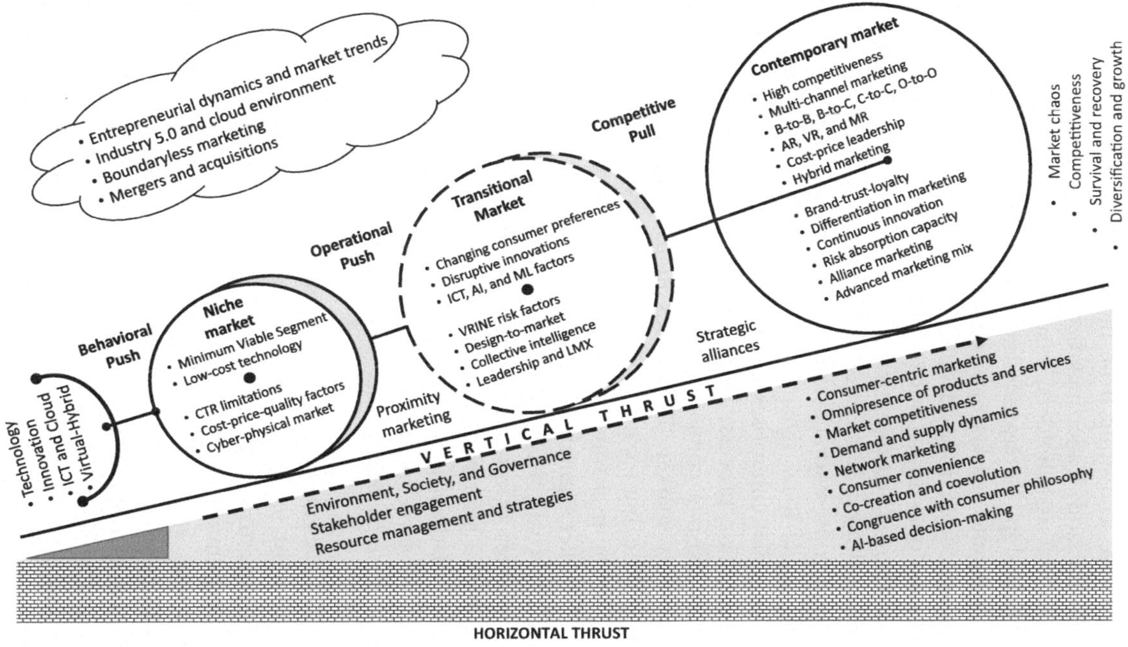

Fig. 1.2 Dynamics of market transition and competitiveness (*Source* Authors)

or uniqueness, assuring inimitability of products and services, non-substitutability, and developing competitive strategies to exploit available market demand. Transiting from niche market, these firms require effective leadership and leader-member exchange (LMX) to engage internal and external stakeholders, manage collective intelligence, and develop cost-leadership. Enterprises transiting from niche market focus on advanced proximity marketing strategies to increase the customer outreach and gain competitive advantage as exhibited in Fig. 1.2. The behavioral push and operational push of niche enterprises develop vertical thrust to move their marketing strategies to match with the contemporary market attributes. It is often a symbiotic relationship between niche markets and contemporary large markets, which can be commonly understood as global–local dynamics. Consequently, large companies often depend on small enterprises as supply agents and engage them in consortium production process. Due to such relationship among these enterprises, there exists a competitive pull across large and small firms in the contemporary market. Enterprises in the contemporary market need to demonstrate high competitiveness to establish corporate and brand image. The multi-channel marketing across B-to-B, B-to-C, C-to-C, and O-to-O market segments is largely practiced as hybrid marketing by developing the cost-price leadership. As discussed in the pre-text, contemporary market offers competitive advantage to the enterprises, which are engaged in improving their marketing efficiency using AR and VR technological platforms. Small enterprises also support their partner enterprises in developing marketing technology platforms including the transcending interest of large firms in working through the metaverse reality platforms.

One of the major challenges in the contemporary market is to develop consistent brand-trust loyalty among internal (employees) and external (consumers and investors) stakeholders by establishing differentiation in marketing and continuous innovation. It is necessary for the transiting niche enterprises to enhance the risk absorption capacity to adapt to advances in marketing technology. Therefore, small and medium enterprises need to explore opportunities of alliance marketing in collaboration with large firms. The alliances can be established in four broad categories comprising production, distribution, technology, and finance segments. Niche enterprises need to develop strategies of advanced marketing mix to gain market competitiveness in the market. The above discussion synthesizes the vertical thrust in the evolution of entrepreneurship driven by the behavioral push (niche market), operation push (transitional market), and competitive pull of the contemporary market. Due to large number of micro, small, and medium enterprises emerging in various sectors in developing countries, there is a mixed defect of success and failures due to increasing chaos in market because of influx of frugal innovative products. These products are not often congruent with the consumer preferences, which reduces the market competitiveness of the products of micro, small, and medium enterprises causing the susceptibility to failure. Consequently, survival and recovery of micro, small, and medium enterprises have been one of the major challenges invoked by rapidly changing technology. Such situation demands these enterprises to diversify their products- and services-mix and stay competitive in the market. The market ecosystem is largely governed by the evolutions in technology and industry, which triggers entrepreneurial dynamics and set new market trends. The advancement in marketing technology has encouraged e-commerce in a cloud environment leading to boundaryless marketing and increasing the consumer outreach.

The elements of horizontal thrust of entrepreneurial transition have been explained in Fig. 1.2, which highlights the stakeholder management as a successful strategy to make collective decisions towards resource management and developing competitive strategies. Besides the consumer-centric marketing through multi-channel strategy, the micro, small, and medium enterprises need to cater to environment, society, and governance requirements to develop a strategy cube comprising design-to-market, design-to-society, and design-to-value (Rajagopal, 2021a). The demand and supply dynamics often control the market competitiveness. Network marketing helps these enterprises in co-creation of designs and co-evolving business with stakeholders and business partners using AL and ML decision making in developing competitive strategies.

Achieving technology-led market competitiveness is complex due to increasing disruptive innovations, changing consumer preferences, and growing alliances between large firms and low-cost manufacturing and supply chain enterprises. Such complex market environments are developed through a combination of cyber-physical interactions in co-creating innovations, co-designing strategies, and co-evolving processes between global and local firms. The transfer of knowledge and technology has played critical role in enhancing capabilities and competencies of local firms to pair up their operational abilities with the large firms. Consequently, the market competitiveness of large firms has significantly increased with the trending ideas, leadership, and organizational excellence (Govindarajan & Trimble, 2005). The market competitiveness of firms today is synchronized with organizational capabilities, which exhibit technology-led mission and vision, strategic objectives to cater to changing markets. The competing firms periodically analyze the internal capabilities and competencies to bridge the tangible and intangible operations systems and simplify administrative processes to facilitate the CTR factors and consumer convenience. The dynamic capabilities of enterprises such as tactical, disruptive, hybrid, and customer-centric approaches contribute significantly to enhance the market competitiveness (Douglas & Craig, 2011). However, achieving consistency in competitive advantage is always obscure in many enterprises as they lack in establishing sustainable differentiation and autonomy among the managers to make timely appropriate decisions. In addition, market competitiveness is largely subjective to the successful implementation of advanced marketing-mix strategies of 11Ps (Rajagopal, 2019), comprising product (differentiation), price (competitive), place (omnipresence), promotion (value oriented), packaging (attractive and cost effective), pace (first mover advantage), people (proximity to customers), performance (product-mix experience), psychodynamics (Customer-to-Customer, collective intelligence, and crowd behavior), posture (corporate and brand image), and proliferation (diversification of portfolios and markets).

A Face in the Niche

Marketing experience of most micro, small, and medium enterprises evolves from the geo-demographic niche, which is differentiated by the consumer preferences, adaptation behavior towards changing technology, and experiencing the perceived value of technology-led innovations. The boom of low-cost technologies has significantly encouraged local enterprises to develop innovation enclaves across the geo-demographic segment that are sensitive to price, quality, and perceived values of products and services. Niche marketing strategy has outgrown as one of the popular conventional marketing designs. Niches or minimum viable segments in traditional market settings focus on a narrow share of the total market pie and operate on lower costs as compared to the large companies. The niche markets operate within unique preferences and cater to the needs of a narrow, well-defined group of buyers better than the potential rivals (Toften & Hammervoll, 2013). The entrepreneurial perception on the CTR factors is gradually declining in niche markets due to increasing customer networking and diffusion of collective intelligence. This phenomenon has supported higher engagement of entrepreneurs with technology by inculcating the sense of low risk in adapting to new technologies and marketing of innovative products and services. Consequently, local innovations with low cost in manufacturing and high affordability in consumption have become attractive in niche markets. The technology and innovative base solutions have increased market competitiveness within and outside the niche markets with increasing product awareness in trial responses at local retail stores. Such development in niche markets has encouraged proactive strategies to counter the increasing competition and establish cost-price-quality matrix to override the high-value brands and aggressive marketing strategies of competing brands. The niche market is developed with distinctive attributes comprising customer centricity, quick and cost-effective supply chain, customer interactivity at various levels, augmented product services, and complementarity with existing products (Ottosson & Kindström, 2016). However, niche markets face oligopolistic market competition, where each enterprise operates in a niche of similar or identical product portfolios, causing chaos across geo-demographic segments. With the increasing technology-led micro and small enterprises, such business scenario is creating congestion in cyber-physical market space. Therefore, these enterprises have adapted to hybrid market approach, which offers physical evidence of enterprise in niche market and helps them to operate in virtual marketplace as well. Connecting niche market with virtual marketspace (e-commerce) causes hypermarket competition across asymmetric consumer behavior (Rajagopal, 2020).

Niche strategies provide a classic instance of such situations. No market is entirely homogeneous. There are always groups of customers that differ in terms of their needs. The possibility of the occurrence of niches, which individual competitors may occupy, always exists. Niches are unlikely to be complete, separate, and well defined. There is always some overlap. However, if such niches are rather subtly defined, they may not always be obvious to all the players. Therefore, niche players may appear to compete. But in practice, they do not do so or at least not fully (Rajagopal, 2016).

The technology enterprises have often moved beyond their niche to share consumer experiences and do business in new order markets overriding the niche scale economy and conceptualizing virtual marketing strategy. The technology-innovation system is characterized by the increasing market shares and quick lifecycle phase, which required a wider market space than marketing in minimum viable segment. The niche market has an interplay of various structural components like knowledge management, financial investment, market access, and technology efficiency, which are often difficult to respond positively within a confined marketplace. These factors potentially determine the control and formation of market systems, which are specific to the consumer preferences within the niche. Therefore, niche markets of technology products cause high risk, low profitability, and narrow scope of expansion of territorial markets. The simple solution to overcome the niche limitations is to adapt to e-commerce in a boundaryless cyberspace (Musiolik et al., 2020). The area of operation or the size of the market does not determine the consumer responsiveness today and the effectiveness of delivery of goods and services in virtual market space. Thus, an entrepreneur in the niche market may just stand as a follower in cyber-physical market competition. Micro, small, and medium firms, therefore, collaborate with large firms with an increasing interest of transforming small area of operation to boundaryless business.

The niche strategy is initially profitable for the enterprises with low total market share. The main reason is that the niche strategy provides total knowledge about the customer segment to the company to enable it to serve better through value addition. In order to gain competitive advantage, firms tend to make their niche market stronger and protected through product, brand, and services differentiation and clear geo-demographic segmentation. Mobile phone companies operate in niche for a longer period and later open their products and services to regional markets. Large companies develop their market initially to serve homogeneous demand and focus on achieving the economy of scale through mass production and mass marketing strategies. These companies tend to control costs through product and services standardization, operating in large market size, and adapting to the principle of systems thinking in 'design-to-market' and systems selling processes. However, the existing market developed by large companies begins fragmenting into the product-specific or geo-demographic niches as the frugal innovations, low-price products, and customization practices grow in the local markets.

Consequently, the large companies realize incremental increase in the operations costs. Such business scenarios might trigger mergers and acquisitions of companies to manage further entropy in business and defection of consumers from the leading brands (Rajagopal, 2021a, 2021b).

Entrepreneurial Domains

Entrepreneurship is evolved within the social, economic, and business ecosystems. The grassroots of entrepreneurship are embedded in social values, ethnicity, and culture, which is influenced by the market trends and consumer preferences over time to develop symbiosis and congruence (Rey-Martí et al., 2016). Therefore, the elements of society constitute a fundamental domain for micro, small, and medium enterprises to evolve as a social value provider and support the social economy. Local enterprises tend to give back to the society by creating employment and strengthening economic contributions. However, entrepreneurship in general is difficult to explain about social outreach with benefits of economy, ecology, environment, and quality of life in the long run. To establish the growth-oriented entrepreneurial domains, it is necessary to identify its contribution to society, innovation, technology, and commercialization. The business being one of the most challenging and fragile domains of entrepreneurship converting entrepreneurial innovations into a marketable products or service. Consequently, to create a small entrepreneurial firm obtaining resources, developing competitiveness, and ensuring a steady growth and survival are difficult propositions in a competitive market environment. Micro, small, and medium enterprises largely evolve around family businesses require a formal business education and strategy to develop entrepreneurial knowledge and skills to stay competitive in the marketplace. The resource management in these enterprises is another major challenge, which requires financial support through open market, strategic alliances, or through public policies (Méndez-Picazo et al., 2012). The governments help in improving economic growth, investment, and business climate among entrepreneurs across the geo-economic territories to create sustainable competitive advantage. In competitive markets, enterprises evolved on the social, economic, corporate, market, technology, and public policy domains stay competitive and survive the market turbulences (Simón-Moya et al., 2012).

Individuals within a social community share certain values, knowledge, collective know-hows, and idiosyncrasies. The collective awareness and idiosyncrasies are linked to social consciousness, and it is intertwined with self-consciousness and the social-self-concept. It is difficult for people to view these attributes separately from the society. The compatibility of an individual's intrinsic moral values with the collective values of the society generates social consciousness such as family values, religious upbringing, social biases, and cultural beliefs (Parris & McInnis-Bowers, 2017). Business models based on social consciousness are influenced by the social factors, which empower entrepreneurial firms to engage customers and stakeholders in entrepreneurial policies. Social consciousness has a profound impact on entrepreneurs as it allows local and small entrepreneurs to collaborate with large industries. Such alliance permits micro, small, and medium enterprises to improve their internal policies, sales strategies, and operations management to gain sustainable growth opportunities in the marketplace. Social consciousness drives the attention of consumers towards conscious consumerism and inclusive businesses with an objective to not only improve the product offering, but also educate consumers and market (Subramanian, 2017).

Family business as a basic domain of entrepreneurship, it is challenging to develop socially constructed business model relevant to competitive marketplace. The family-based enterprises evolve within the socio-historical domain through learnt management insights, which is often non-congruent with current market trends to contribute to a successful business formation. Over time, the decline of multi-generational families, growing market competition, and increasing occupational opportunities outside the enterprise weakens the foundation of the family business entrepreneurial learning. In industrial capitalism and massive transformations in the family formation and compositions, entrepreneurs are bound to seek market resources such as human capital, financial capital, technology, and managerial know-how. The new market order has induced interdependence across the enterprises irrespective of their sizes to gain market competitiveness, manage the CTR limits, and achieve competitive advantages. The market fragmentation and diverse consumer preferences have encouraged diversity in products and services, and geographic markets. In emerging economies, family and public participation in entrepreneurial development has been supported by public policies and community upliftment programs. Such programs build capacity in the community to improve economic self-sufficiency and freedom among enterprises through active participation at niche level. In addition to the entrepreneurial expectations, technology learning, and managerial mindset, affect entrepreneurial competitiveness in the marketplace (Wang et al., 2021). Recently, reverse entrepreneurship has encountered an increase in their caregiving roles and responsibilities, which has increased the collaborative opportunities within the industrial network. This has stimulated the entrepreneurial infrastructure in developing countries towards management of innovative enterprises. Some developed nations have implemented long-term paternity leaves, flexible work arrangement, and diversity and inclusion strategies to support entrepreneurial workforce. Such public policies encourage workplace professionalism and transgenerational leadership in improving the local economy. This situation has encouraged entrepreneurs to improve their productivity through innovation and technology and match their products and services with market offering (Rajagopal, 2021b). Consequently, the social and political change has been favorable to overcome the conventional barriers and promote a successful and dynamic economic growth of micro, small, and medium enterprises.

Broadly, the entrepreneurial domains can be identified within the operational ecosystem involving personality traits of entrepreneurs, community coordination, social and ethical aspects, industry attractiveness, and the public policies to encourage micro, small, and medium enterprises. The public policy plays specific role in supporting entrepreneurship by providing financial support and skill development to acquire innovation and technology. Successful enterprises with public policy support emerge as innovators and gain the capability of disrupting existing markets with innovative products and services (Pankov et al., 2019). The other domains of entrepreneurship, which drive success through market competitiveness, include disruptive marketing practices, business incubation, business networking, entrepreneurial education, and enterprise infrastructure. Consequently, entrepreneurial domains, which are derived from entrepreneurial ecosystem, involve multilevel entrepreneurial processes, stakeholders, players, and manufacturing and marketing across diverse entrepreneurial activities. These factors are significantly affected by the accessibility (geographical and physical distance), infrastructure, and available resources among entrepreneurs and market outreach. The entrepreneurial domains are complex and diverse, which are often managed through personal, social, and corporate relationships to determine the success of enterprises. The entrepreneurial ecosystem is, therefore, a combination of human interactive elements comprising social and industrial networks, shared values, shared economy, and consortium production practices. The entrepreneurial domains have both tangible and intangible systems that can be understood through the existing resources, knowledge and skills, public policy support, and competitive advantage. These active domains help enterprises to achieve competitive advantage and ability in scaling the enterprises (Spigel, 2017). The Schumpeterian arguments on entrepreneurial domains endorse the impact of different innovation policies on the short- and long-run entrepreneurial performance through the attributes of public economy and policy. The innovation policies broadly refer to the new knowledge, new products, and efficient production techniques that help enterprises to achieve market competitiveness. The entrepreneurial growth depends on the scope of public policy tools employed by developing economies, which affects the entrepreneurial market and economy. The public policies to support local enterprises must focus on technological renewal and market-driven innovation to reduce the CTR effects and improve business breakeven to gain competitive advantage. Such policy support needs to be diffusion oriented and co-create entrepreneurial processes to institutionalize the entrepreneurship at the grassroots and beyond (Mazzucato & Semieniuk, 2017).

In context of the conventional small enterprises, entrepreneurship is a process of slow business performance within a niche, which can be easily predicted. However, the changing technology and innovation demand strategic renewal of manufacturing, servitization, and marketing approach of these enterprises. The development of an existing business through the creation of new products, services, and activities; and building resistance to new competitive threats in the market call for strategic approaches to growth. The strategic approaches of small enterprises are implemented through systems thinking. The strategic enterprise process allows the enterprises to co-evolve with other enterprises, stakeholders, or entrepreneurial gatekeepers. Thus, small enterprises are investing on strategic business models through building managerial capabilities to unfold the latent entrepreneurial potential. Frugal innovation, co-evolution of reverse innovation business designs, development of participatory innovation models, and collective intelligence (crowdsourcing) offer new insights to small enterprises and enable them to gain corporate entrepreneurship (Elia & Margherita, 2018). Micro, small, and medium enterprises need to be supported by the public policies to operate in niche, but tend to expand access to capital, increase intellectual-property protections, learn modern entrepreneurism, and update on financial regulations. These initiatives drive intensive efforts by policy-makers, business leaders, and entrepreneurs to augment the social and economic performance of small enterprises. Consequently, public policies and consortium production model of large companies put forward a new growth formula that complements the conventional enterprise model and builds a sustainable future. The boom of software enterprises has substantially exploited the growth of technology, and the start-up enterprises have taken the maximum share of this technological growth in emerging markets. Entrepreneurship in information technology-based enterprises has grown manifold and yet to reach far in the cyberspace (Rajagopal, 2021a, 2021b).

References

Acs, Z. J., & Mueller, P. (2007). Employment effects of business dynamics: Mice, gazelles and elephants. *Small Business Economics, 30*(1), 85–100.

Ahn, S., Kim, K.-S., & Lee, K.-H. (2022). Technological Capabilities, Entrepreneurship and Innovation of Technology-Based Start-Ups: The Resource-Based View. *Journal of Open Innovation: Technology, Market, and Complexity, 8*(3), 156–172.

Audretsch, D. B., Bönte, W., & Keilbach, M. (2008). Entrepreneurship capital and its impact on knowledge diffusion and economic performance. *Journal of Business Venturing, 23*(6), 687–698.

Bosco, B. D., Chierici, R., & Mazzucchelli, A. (2019). Fostering entrepreneurship: An innovative business model to link innovation and new venture creation. *Review of Management Science, 13*(2019), 561–574. https://doi.org/10.1007/s11846-018-0318-8

Camisón-Haba, S., Clemente-Almendros, J. A., & González-Cruz, T. (2019). How technology-based firms become also highly innovative firms? The role of knowledge, technological and managerial capabilities, and entrepreneurs' background. *Journal of Innovation & Knowledge, 4*(3), 162–170.

Carayannis, E. G., Dezi, L., Gregori, G., & Calo, E. (2021). Smart environments and techno-centric and human-centric innovations for industry and society 5.0: A quintuple helix innovation system view towards smart, sustainable, and inclusive solutions. *Journal of the Knowledge Economy, 13*, 926–955.

Chaudhry, S., Crick, D., & Crick, J. M. (2024). Technology oriented, service intensive, transnational entrepreneurs' international target market strategies. *Industrial Marketing Management, 120*, 175–190.

Douglas, S. P., & Craig, C. S. (2011). Convergence and divergence: Developing a semiglobal marketing strategy. *Journal of International Marketing, 19*(1), 82–101.

Elia, G., & Margherita, A. (2018). Assessing the maturity of crowdventuring for corporate entrepreneurship. *Business Horizons, 61*(2), 271–283.

Eng, T.-Y., & Ozdemir, S. (2014). Internal R&D partnerships and intrafirm R&D-marketing-production integration of manufacturing firms in emerging economies. *Industrial Marketing Management, 43*(1), 32–44.

Gabrielsson, M., Seppälä, T., & Gabrielsson, P. (2016). Realizing a hybrid competitive strategy and achieving superior financial performance while internationalizing in the high-technology market. *Industrial Marketing Management, 54*, 141–153.

Gao, P., Kaas, H. W., Mohr, D., & Wee, D. (2016). *Disruptive trends that will transform the auto industry*. Industry Report. New York: McKinsey and Company.

Giasolli, R., Groen, A., Haak, R., & Pieck, M. (2021). Identifying management of technology and innovation (MOT) and technology entrepreneurship (TE) centers of excellence. *Technological Forecasting and Social Change*, 173. https://doi.org/10.1016/j.techfore.2021.121075

Govindarajan, V., & Trimble, C. (2005). Building breakthrough businesses within established organizations. *Harvard Business Review, 83*(5), 58–68.

Harrison, R. L., III., Thomas, K. D., & Cross, S. N. N. (2017). Restricted visions 330 of multiracial identity in advertising. *Journal of Advertising, 46*(4), 503–520.

Hedaa, L., & Ritter, T. (2005). Business relationships on different waves: Paradigm shift and marketing orientation revisited. *Industrial Marketing Management., 34*(7), 714–721.

Hughes, M., Martin, S. L., Morgan, R. E., & Robson, M. J. (2010). Realizing product-market advantage in high-technology international new ventures: The mediating role of ambidextrous innovation. *Journal of International Marketing, 18*(4), 1–21.

Koo, W. W., & Eesley, C. E. (2021). Platform governance and the rural–urban divide: Sellers' responses to design change. *Strategic Management Journal, 42*(5), 941–967.

Lee, M. T., Raschke, R. L., & Krishen, A. S. (2022). Signaling green! Firm ESG signals in an interconnected environment that promote brand valuation. *Journal of Business Research, 138*, 1–11.

Leyden, D. P., & Link, A. N. (2015). Toward a theory of the entrepreneurial process. *Small Business Economics, 44*, 475–484.

Leng, J., Zhong, Y., Lin, Z., Xu, K., Mourtzis, D., Zhou, X., Zheng, P., Liu, Q., Zhao, J. L., & Shen, W. (2023). Towards resilience in Industry 5.0: A decentralized autonomous manufacturing paradigm. *Journal of Manufacturing Systems, 71*, 95–114.

Licsandru, T. C., & Cui, C. C. (2019). Ethnic marketing to the global millennial consumers: Challenges and opportunities. *Journal of Business Research, 103*, 261–274.

Méndez-Picazo, M. T., Galindo-Martín, M. Á., & Ribeiro-Soriano, D. (2012). Governance, entrepreneurship and economic growth. *Entrepreneurship and Regional Development, 24*(9–10), 865–877.

Musiolik, J., Markard, J., Hekkert, M., & Furrer, B. (2020). Creating innovation systems: How resource constellations affect the strategies of system builders. *Technological Forecasting and Social Change*, 153. https://doi.org/10.1016/j.techfore.2018.02.002

Mazzucato, M., & Semieniuk, G. (2017). Public financing of innovation: New questions. *Oxford Review of Economic Policy, 33*(1), 24–48.

Ottosson, M., & Kindström, D. (2016). Exploring proactive niche market strategies in the steel industry: Activities and implications. *Industrial Marketing Management, 55*, 119–130.

Ouahabi, N., Chebak, A., Kamach, O., Laayati, O., & Zegrari, M. (2024). Leveraging digital twin into dynamic production scheduling: A review. *Robotics and Computer-Integrated Manufacturing*, 89. https://doi.org/10.1016/j.rcim.2024.102778

Pankov, S., Velamuri, V. K., & Schneckenberg, D. (2019). Towards sustainable entrepreneurial ecosystems: Examining the effect of contextual factors on sustainable entrepreneurial activities in the sharing economy. *Small Business Economics, 56*, 1073–1095.

Parris, D. L., & McInnis-Bowers, C. (2017). Business not as usual: Developing socially conscious entrepreneurs and intrapreneurs. *Journal of Management Education., 41*(5), 687–726.

Prashantham, S., & Yip, G. S. (2016). Engaging with startups in emerging markets. *MIT Sloan Management Review, 55*(4), 27–34.

Pustovrh, A., Rangus, K., & Drnovšek, M. (2020). The role of open innovation in developing an entrepreneurial support ecosystem. *Technology Forecasting and Social Change*, 152. https://doi.org/10.1016/j.techfore.2019.119892

Maddikunta, P. K. R., Pham, Q.-V., Prabadevi, B., Deepa, N., Dev, K., Gadekallu, T. R., Ruby, R., & Liyanage, M. (2022). Industry 5.0: A survey on enabling technologies and potential applications. *Journal of Industrial Information Integration*, 26. https://doi.org/10.1016/j.jii.2021.100257.

Rajagopal. (2016). *Sustainable growth in global markets: Strategic choices and managerial implications*. Palgrave Macmillan.

Rajagopal. (2019). *Contemporary marketing strategy: Analyzing consumer behavior to drive managerial decision making*. Palgrave Macmillan.

Rajagopal. (2020). *Market entropy: How to manage chaos and uncertainty for improving organizational performance*. Business Expert Press.

Rajagopal. (2021a). *The business design cube: Converging markets, society, and customer values to grow competitive in business*. Business Expert Press.

Rajagopal. (2021b). Entrepreneurial strategies, managerial implications, prospects, and dilemmas. In Rajagopal & R. Behl (Eds.), *Entrepreneurship and regional development: Analyzing growth models in emerging markets*. Palgrave Macmillan.

Rajagopal. (2022). *Agile marketing strategies—New approaches to engaging consumer behavior*. Springer.

Rajagopal. (2024). *Rebuilding entrepreneurship at the grassroots: Converging divergent factors of society and economy*. Springer, Palgrave Macmillan.

Ratten, V., & Jones, P. (2021). Entrepreneurship and management education: Exploring trends and gaps. *International Journal of Management in Education, 19*(1), Art. 100431. https://doi.org/10.1016/j.ijme.2020.10043

Rey-Martí, A., Ribeiro-Soriano, D., & Sánchez-García, J. L. (2016). Giving back to society: Job creation through social entrepreneurship. *Journal of Business Research, 69*(6), 2067–2072.

Salamzadeh, A., Radovic, M. M., & Salamzadeh, Y. (2022). The economic resilience-entrepreneurship nexus. *Journal of Entrepreneurship and Business Resilience, 5*(1), 7–12.

Seungku, A., Kwon-Sik, K., & Kwang-Hoon, L. (2022). Technological capabilities, entrepreneurship and innovation of technology-based start-ups: The resource-based view. *Journal of Open Innovation: Technology, Market, and Complexity, 8*(3), Art. 156. https://doi.org/10.3390/joitmc8030156

Simón-Moya, V., Revuelto-Taboada, L., & Ribeiro-Soriano, D. (2012). Are success and survival factors the same for social and business ventures? *Service Business, 6*(2), 219–242.

Spigel, B. (2017). The relational organization of entrepreneurial ecosystems. *Entrepreneurship Theory and Practice, 41*(1), 49–72.

Subramanian, K. R. (2017). Social consciousness and indifferent business postures. *Journal of Advance Research in Business, Management and Accounting, 3*(6), 1–12.

Symeonidou, N., DeTienne, D. R., & Chirico, F. (2022). The persistence of family firms: How does performance threshold affect family firm exit? *Small Business Economics, 59*, 477–489.

Tsai, K.-H., & Hsu, T. T. (2014). Cross-functional collaboration, competitive intensity, knowledge integration mechanisms, and new product performance: A mediated moderation model. *Industrial Marketing Management, 43*(2), 293–303.

Toften, K., & Hammervoll, T. (2013). Niche marketing research: Status and challenges. *Marketing Intelligence and Planning, 31*(3), 272–285.

Tomizawa, A., Zhao, L., Bassellier, G., & Ahlstrom, D. (2020). Economic growth, innovation, institutions, and the Great Enrichment. *Asia Pacific Journal of Management, 37*(1), 7–31.

Tong Qin, T. W., & Liu, R. R. (2019). The impact of nostalgic emotion on brand trust and brand attachment: An empirical study from China. *Asia Pacific Journal of Marketing and Logistics, 31*(4), 1118–1137.

Veloutsou, C., Chatzipanagiotou, K., & Christodoulides, G. (2020). The consumer-based brand equity deconstruction and restoration process: Lessons from unliked brands. *Journal of Business Research, 111*, 41–51.

Wang, S., Wan, J., Zhang, D., Li, D., & Zhang, C. (2016). Towards smart factory for industry 4.0: A self-organized multi-agent system with big data based feedback and coordination. *Computer Networks, 101*, 158–168.

Wang, Q., dt ogilvie, & Richardson, L. (2021). Race/ethnicity, place, and art and culture entrepreneurship in underserved communities, Cities, 115. https://doi.org/10.1016/j.cities.2021.103243

Wu, X., Wu, Z., & Hu, J. (2022). Global competitiveness analysis of industrial robot technology innovations market layout using visibility graph. *Physica A: Statistical Mechanics and its Applications*, 603. https://doi.org/10.1016/j.physa.2022.127672

Wurth, B., Stam, E., & Spigel, B. (2021). Toward an entrepreneurial ecosystem research program. *Entrepreneurship Theory and Practice, 46*(3), 729–778.

Xu, X., Lu, Y., Vogel-Heuser, B., & Wang, L. (2021). Industry 4.0 and Industry 5.0—Inception, conception and perception. *Journal of Manufacturing Systems, 61*, 530–535.

Zahra, S. A. (2021). The resource-based view, resourcefulness, and resource management in startup firms: A proposed research agenda. *Journal of Management, 47*, 1841–1860.

Zhou, J., Zhou, Y., Wang, B., & Zang, J. (2019). Human–cyber–physical systems (HCPSs) in the context of new-generation intelligent manufacturing. *Engineering, 5*, 624–636.

CHAPTER 2

Contextualizing Entrepreneurship with Society and Business

Abstract This chapter presents discussions on the attributes and consequences of systems thinking on enhancing the efficiency of entrepreneurship within the social and economic challenges. The market consciousness, innovation perspective, and consumer value creation as the tools for social proximity and crowd-based business modeling have also been discussed in this chapter. Contextualizing entrepreneurship with society and business discussions in this chapter focuses on enhancing social proximity of micro, small, and medium enterprises to develop interaction with internal and external stakeholders. The discussions argue that social proximity will help in developing crowd-based business model and carrying out open innovations. In addition, the MIC factors comprising market consciousness, innovation perspectives, and creating consumer value have been discussed in this chapter. Discussion on advances in digital technologies, which have increased the possibilities of open innovation and outsourcing entrepreneurial activities to explore new opportunities, has also added value to this chapter.

Keywords Systems thinking · Knowledge management · Social proximity · Prismatic structure · Crowd-based business modeling · Market consciousness · Innovation perspectives · Consumer value creation

Rajagopal and A. Rajagopal, *Unmasking Invisible Challenges in Entrepreneurship*, Palgrave Studies of Entrepreneurship and Social Challenges in Developing Economies,
https://doi.org/10.1007/978-3-031-63653-0_2

The genesis of entrepreneurship is based on society and family values while being nurtured within the business ecosystem adapting to the market requirements and consumer preferences. Local enterprises evolve by understanding the problems, needs, and solutions factors (PNS) and analyzing the complexities in the society. These enterprises largely cater to the social needs overlooking the prospects of commercialization and investing in continuous innovation and technology to stay competitive in the marketplace (Aparicio et al., 2016). The micro, small, and medium enterprises grow social as they obtain local resources and operationalize their enterprise within the social and economic limitations. However, these enterprises manifest capabilities and competencies to increase social proximity, perceive and create new economic opportunities, develop innovative products, and introduce frugal innovative ideas in market. As these enterprises operate on conventional knowledge and skills, their market competitiveness is often affected due to lack of scaling of business and weak entrepreneurial design to match with the cost, time, and risk (CTR) factors. Despite the embedded weaknesses contextual to society and business, the innovative micro enterprises have emerged as a critical role player in contributing to the local economy (Porfirio et al., 2016). Consequently, urban-oriented entrepreneurs start micro enterprises to explore market opportunities by estimating the probable risks, operational complexities, and paucity of resources. These factors affect the size of these enterprises and limit their operations in large market ecosystems. Increasing social consciousness and public policy support has enhanced the training and educational attainment among entrepreneurs of micro, small, and medium enterprises to improve their management capability. General business knowledge and formal education have significantly influenced entrepreneurs to contribute to the innovative ventures and develop market competitiveness. These factors have inculcated systems thinking in micro, small, and medium enterprises to develop compatibility with the changing business environment, technology, and operational practices.

Systems Thinking

Systems thinking converges social and market-driven entrepreneurial requirement by emphasizing the required knowledge and skills and an overreaching mindset to build their enterprise by analyzing the PNS factors. The problems can be effectively solved by considering the social, economic, technological, and market-based relationships (Hyytinen,

2021). Most enterprises at the grassroots have evolved within the closed knowledge systems, which often prevented learning, experimenting, and experiencing new concepts (Judge, 2011). Consequently, most enterprises at the local level were pushed into socio-economic cocoons, which closed their boundaries to reach urban markets and develop competitiveness across products, brands, and services. Systems thinking is a continuous learning process, which has revolutionized the entrepreneurial management practices by challenging the conventional potholes. The continuous learning is encouraged by observing the changing entrepreneurial practices and their adaptability to explore opportunities and stay competitive in the marketplace. The systems thinking in entrepreneurship transcends operational practices, design thinking, and interorganizational symbiosis to identify strengths and opportunities to overcome the embedded weaknesses in the entrepreneurial practices and external threats. Systems thinking is a self-learning concept in which entrepreneurs need to identify the risks and diversify their part to evade any operational jeopardy. Systems thinking requires entrepreneurs to consider innovation and technology subsystems, and managerial components within the organization to develop congruence with a larger business ecosystem. However, systems thinking varies by the size of enterprises, which requires appropriate resource allocations to develop a balanced learning and possibilities to adapt the new concepts of successful enterprises (Kapasi & Rosli, 2020).

Systems consist of people, structures, technologies, and processes that work together to make organizations viable. Systems thinking, a part of operations and management research, essentially looks at the whole as a basis for understanding, designing, and managing its components. Systems thinking has been applied in organizational management for decades in the field of operations and has also been conceptualized in the functional areas of marketing. Systems thinking offers a powerful new perspective, a synchronized flow of thoughts, and a set of tools that can be used to address the most complex problems in everyday business operations. Systems thinking may be considered as a way of understanding reality that emphasizes the relationships among various components in a process, rather than the independent constituents of the process. Based on a field of study known as system dynamics, systems thinking has a practical value that rests on a solid theoretical foundation. In marketing operations, systems thinking can be described as a tool in tracing and linking various activities in a particular function.

To be competitive, companies must develop innovative new businesses though on competitive market platforms. Firms may face several operational barriers and seldom mesh smoothly with well-established systems, processes, and cultures. Nonetheless, success requires a balance of conventional and new marketing strategies to keep the competitive forces in equilibrium (Garvin & Levesque, 2006). Systems thinking requires new mental models of entrepreneurs to consider contemporary assumptions, best practices, experience-based generalizations, and customer influences to develop pro-innovation and pro-market entrepreneurial practices. Very often, these considerations are not drawn consciously, which affects entrepreneurial mental models and behavior. Therefore, change-capable enterprises are always conscious of their collective mental models and applied learnings.

Emerging companies face various challenges while pursuing new businesses as well as the usual problematic responses to those challenges. The systems thinking is usually driven by many smaller systems or subsystems. For example, an organization is made up of many administrative and management functions, products, services, groups, and individuals. If one part of the system is changed, the nature of the overall system is often changed as well by definition. Systems theory has brought a new perspective for managers to interpret patterns and events in their organizations. The co-evolution of small and big companies enhances investment on innovation, technology, and research and development (Wiklund et al., 2019). Such mergers or acquisitions in the double helix approach help companies strengthen their marketing strategies by developing customer-centric branding and promotion strategies. The convergence of technology, entrepreneurship education, and public policies on entrepreneurship development programs promotes hybridization, business performance, and corporate citizenship behavior ambidextrously between small and large enterprises. The 5-T determinants lay the groundwork for success inside the new organization. The typical work culture of 5-T power-grid may be described as synergy of task (commitment), thrust (driving force) and time (punctuality), target (customers by segments), and trust (value perceptions). These attributes of the Japanese distinguish them from most of the existing work cultures across the countries in the world (Rajagopal, 2021a). This has reflected into the material culture (technology and economy) of Japan towards continues improvement (Kaizen). In fact, Kaizen is a social culture, which has been later adopted by the Japanese organizations. These indicators serve as drivers of systems thinking in business. An appropriate convergence of these factors has made the business firms stronger and sustainable during the economic recessions. It is observed that knowledge management fully mediates the impact of organizational culture on organizational effectiveness and partially mediates the impact of organizational structure and strategy on organizational effectiveness. There is a possible mediating role of knowledge management in managing relationship between the systems thinking attributes comprising organizational goals, employee engagement, stakeholder values, work culture, decision-making process, and organizational effectiveness (Zheng et al., 2010).

With the increasing adaptation of technology in industry 5.0, the need for systems thinking at various levels of operation and sizes of enterprises has become inevitable. Entrepreneurs need to develop different skill sets with applied dimensions to practice systems thinking and develop industry attractiveness and market competitiveness in complex ecosystems. There are various attributes of systems thinking, which are backed by data analytics and collective intelligence in the current environment of virtual business. Systems thinking practices vary across individuals and organization, which impacts entrepreneurial skill sets and organizational behavior in managing work environment, business models, and innovation and technology. Systems thinking helps entrepreneurs in managing calculated risks emerging out of multi-dimensional problems in managing business in competitive environments (Rajagopal, 2021a). Organizations practicing systems thinking prefer to explore a workable solution and explore the surroundings of the business ecosystem. Simplicity and autonomy in enterprises encourage favorable ambience for systems thinking. Accordingly, these attributes help entrepreneurs in self-diagnosis of problems, experiment new models based on best practices, and take independent decisions to improve performance at pilot level prior to generalization. The entrepreneurial autonomy not only encourages independence in thinking, diagnostics, and decision making, but also develops balance between internal autonomy and integration of external attributes related to business performance (Jaradat et al., 2017). The broader perspective of systems thinking leads to global integration, a trend of interdependent decisions to achieve holistic performance. Systems thinking stimulates teamwork process to analyze the entrepreneurial situations collectively using participatory entrepreneurial approach as against rapid entrepreneurial approach practiced individually in isolation (Rajagopal, 2021a). Entrepreneurs can work in small systems and develop cause and effect solution in small experimental teams by establishing coordination, communication, and interconnectedness across the teams. Working in teams reduces the resistance to change and focuses on resolving internal conflicts by working with consensus. Systems thinking helps entrepreneurs to focus on specific indicators of performance and develop systems behavior to experience a holistic view of innovative entrepreneurial paradigm (Chou, 2018). This is a flexible approach under systems thinking process, which opens to new ideas and is motivated by agile plans. However, the complexity level related to problem solving in systems thinking varies at operational and organizational levels. Therefore, it is necessary for entrepreneurs to acquire systems knowledge on different perspectives compatible with rapidly changing business ecosystems (Tazzit et al., 2023). The attributes of systems thinking required in developing entrepreneurship are exhibited in Fig. 2.1.

Most micro, small, and medium enterprises emerging out of family business have shown resistance to change since long in developing economies, as these enterprises are unable to manage the CTR factors as illustrated in Fig. 2.1. The lack of specific awareness about PNS factors increases the resistance to change combined with the paucity of resources and low market proximity as these enterprises largely operate at the niche level. Consequently, systems thinking in entrepreneurship is a topic of right interest in academics and industry to align local enterprises with the upstream markets and develop interdependency between local and large enterprises. Systems thinking has attractive propositions for both entrepreneurs at the grassroots and the enterprise management team to influence organizational culture, behavior, and efficiency in decision making to align local enterprises with the business ecosystem beyond niche environment. Systems thinking has an impact on four entrepreneurial domains comprising entrepreneurship (personality and behavior), knowledge orchestration (continuous learning), organizational perspectives (decision making), and business ecosystem (market dynamics). As grassroots enterprise adapts to socio-economic niche with limited innovation and market outreach, these enterprises operate under closed knowledge (lack of continuity and knowledge updates) and cognition, which encapsulate micro, small, and medium enterprises with conventional entrepreneurial practices. Consequently, these enterprises jeopardize their operational performance leading to slow growth and off-trend image. Local enterprises exhibit enormous, learned competencies as

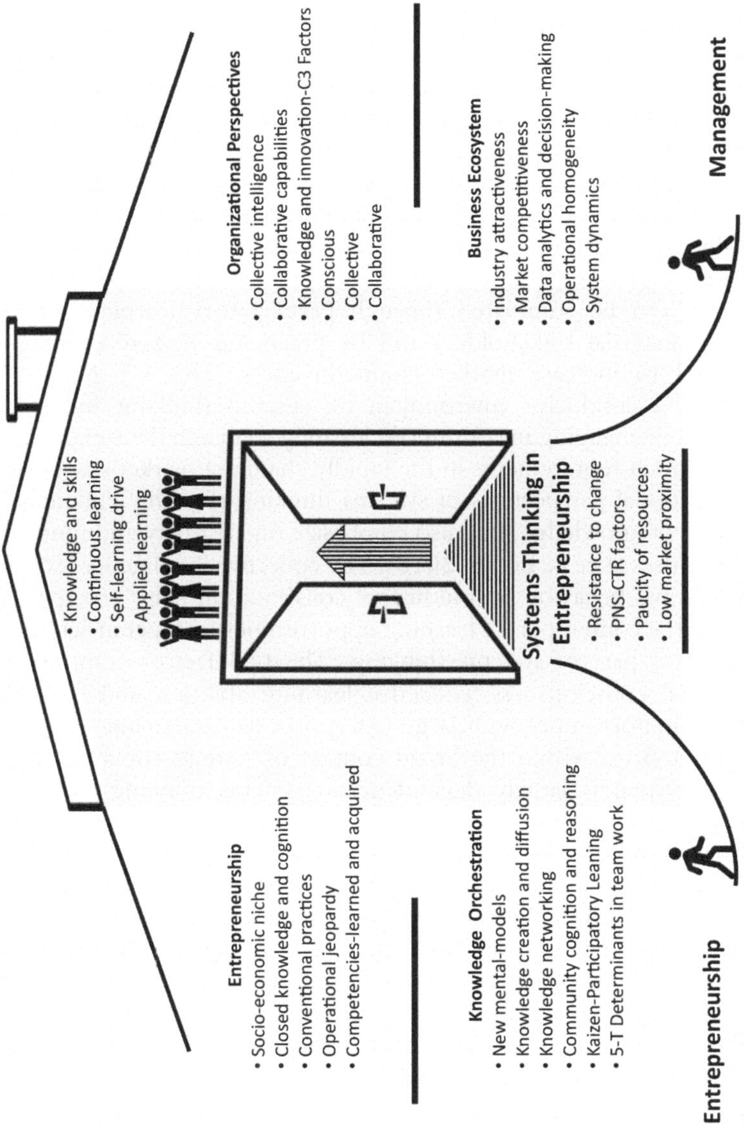

Fig. 2.1 Systems thinking in entrepreneurship (*Source* Authors)

they outgrow family business but significantly lack in acquired knowledge from the contemporary best practices (Ano & Bent, 2022).

Figure 2.1 illustrates that knowledge orchestration is one of the principal contributions of the systems thinking in entrepreneurship, which encourages new mental models through continuous learning, knowledge creation, and diffusion. The knowledge orchestration can be strengthened for micro, small, and medium enterprises within consortiums through knowledge networking. Systems thinking is a continuous learning process, which improves community cognition and the ability of reasoning to adapt to new mental models and stay competitive in the marketplace (Mingjie et al., 2020). The knowledge orchestration in enterprise can be stimulated through participatory learning across internal and external stakeholders and by practicing Kaizen as design thinking tool to increase market competitiveness. The 5-T determinants provide a conducive environment for systems thinking and help entrepreneurs in engaging in continuous learning to match their manufacturing and market requirements in the rapidly changing market scenarios. The organizational perspectives of systems thinking not only encourage enhancement of knowledge, but also emphasize on creativity and innovation in enterprises (Lee & Eesley, 2018). The collective intelligence (social media and crowd behavior) and industrial collaboration helps enterprises in increasing the contemporary learning opportunities, competencies, and capabilities as a part of systems thinking. The C-3 factors comprising entrepreneurial consciousness, collective learning abilities, and seeking collaborative opportunities with large enterprises foster dynamic organizational perspectives within the broad context of systems thinking. The business ecosystem is largely dependent on systems thinking to drive continuous growth among enterprises of different types and sizes. The complexities of industry attractiveness and market competitiveness can be well understood by the firms through systems thinking practices. With the emergence of artificial intelligence (AI), machine learning (ML), and data analytics, decision making has also been a part of sophisticated systems thinking, which helps enterprises in developing operational homogeneity and aligning with the system dynamics of enterprises. Therefore, there is a rush of entrepreneurs and enterprise management teams in learning systems thinking practices to maintain updated knowledge and critical success path in managing enterprises through the business chaos.

Reviewing all the attributes of systems thinking exhibited in Fig. 2.1, it is pertinent that continuous learning in enterprises of different sizes across the geographies helps in improving the knowledge and skills of entrepreneurs to enable them to develop competitive manufacturing, innovation, and marketing plans to stay competitive. Systems thinking encourages self-learning at micro level and in developing analytical cognitive skills to converge knowledge and skills to foster their competitive entrepreneurial and business plans. For adapting systems thinking to organizational culture, it is necessary for enterprises to develop a common skill acquisition platform, which can be developed as hybrid learning centers.

In the competitive business environment, large firms operate with open ecosystems to gain competitive leverage by commercializing open-innovation and reverse-innovation products. This strategy helps firms in delivering high customer value and inculcate perceptions among customers on collective creativity. Consequently, firms can retain the loyalty and support of ecosystem partners and stakeholders to ensure their continued performance in the marketplace. Continuous learning and exploring ways to catch-up with changes in the industry drive firms to stay agile with the dynamic business ecosystems (Rajagopal, 2021a). Industrial marketing firms have moved today from relationship-management goals to ecosystems-orchestration process. Business environment today is hierarchically arrayed within industry with transitional multimodal business system across large firms. Large firms within industries (such as pharmaceuticals) develop business consortiums and focus on collaborative strategizing and expanding the key partners geographically. The changing business ecosystems today drive greater flexibility in strategic partnership by allowing firms to develop collaborations contextual to the collective intelligence, social values, and benefit-spread across the stakeholders (Reeves et al., 2015).

Systems thinking in enterprises is one of the organized approaches to converge the social values with business perspectives to enable entrepreneurs to make decisions in the context of society, values, and market. Assuring organizational performance by using systems thinking approach requires transformational leadership and collaboration within inter- and intra-organizational teams to co-create and co-evolve entrepreneurial plans. Systems thinking is successfully practiced also in hybrid organization, which entails social innovations to co-design business models and implement them through public–private partnership. Enhancing stakeholder value and socializing the enterprises require to develop appropriate systems thinking within enterprises to co-create value through collective innovations, collaborative capabilities, and acquired competencies. Emerging companies face various challenges when they pursue new businesses, as well as the usual problematic responses to those challenges. The systems thinking is usually driven by many smaller systems or subsystems. For example, an organization is made up of many administrative and management functions, products, services, groups, and individuals. If one part of the system is changed, the nature of the overall system is often changed as well by definition. Systems theory has brought a new perspective for managers to interpret patterns and events in their organizations (Rajagopal, 2021a).

Social Proximity

Entrepreneurship at the grassroots and social learning is symbiotic in entrepreneurial ecosystem. Orchestration of customer-centric entrepreneurship is largely influenced by the social learning process, which helps in understanding the embedded PNS factors in the society and to estimate the effectiveness of the elements of CTR metrics. Social learning is a continuous process, which requires considerable proximity of entrepreneurs with the social stakeholders to develop congruence with their needs, changing preferences, and market demand to stay agile with the dynamic ecosystems. The social facet of entrepreneurship is based on personal, social, and crowd-based relationships to develop greater flexibility and collaborations with geo-demographic segments to gain advantage of collective intelligence, social values, and benefit spread across the stakeholders (Reeves et al., 2015). The principal and peripheral attributes of entrepreneurial ecosystem are focused on strategic perspectives of social needs, the changing preferences of stakeholders, and the transcending competition in the marketplace. The notion of social proximity in entrepreneurship addresses the entrepreneurial interdependence with social values and the relative concepts of collaboration and competition such as customer-centric and market-led strategies of business. These factors predominantly affect the dynamism of entrepreneurial and business ecosystems. The social proximity in entrepreneurship is driven by both intrinsic and extrinsic attributes. The intrinsic attributes drive innovations based on family values, experience, social values, and cultural aspects. The entrepreneurial perspectives based on social and market needs broadly constitute the extrinsic attributes, which influence entrepreneurial growth and performance.

The social and market-based entrepreneurial strategies not only benefit from the social proximity, but also help entrepreneurs to gain competitive advantage by exploring opportunities beyond niche and strengthen their business within the oligopolistic market system. The social business philosophy of entrepreneurship bridges conventional and contemporary business practices by integrating innovation and technology within the social and cultural values (Parente et al., 2018). Traditional firms considered macro elements in the business as exogenous drivers of business ecosystem and focused on controllable variables like organizational design, work culture, and marketing-mix. Entrepreneurial proximity to society and market helps in continuous learning about the dynamics of exogenous elements like competitors, suppliers, stakeholders, and business partners which have become endogenous management factors of the business ecosystem. Social proximity, crowd behavior, and collective intelligence influence innovation and technology, which contributes to a competitive business environment today. Accordingly, entrepreneurship at the grassroots level is evolving with factors concerning customer-related attributes, leading to agile entrepreneurship. The multilateral factors in the business ecosystem include government, business partners (manufacturing, logistics, and marketing), financial institutions, and information technology providers. The contemporary marketing philosophy is founded on a polyhedron framework that has a triangular prismatic effect with five faces, six edges, and nine vertices. The philosophical thoughts on modern business can be stretched wide from the geometric structure to the functional propositions in the marketplace, which entails broadly the market, society, and customer values (Rajagopal, 2024).

The social proximity in entrepreneurship constitutes one of the edges of prismatic structure of entrepreneurial management. The broad view of prismatic structure of entrepreneurial management can be viewed with five faces, six edges, and nine vertices, which helps entrepreneurs in developing their entrepreneurial model. The faces of prismatic structure of entrepreneurial management consist of manufacturing (conventional practices, community infrastructure, and design thinking), resource mapping (capital and human resources, raw material, and suppliers), innovation (frugal, bricolage, experiential, cultural, and ethnic), technology (CTR factors, adaptability, and awareness), and stakeholders (angel investors, consumers, geo-demographic segments, and value perspectives). There are six edges encompassing knowledge management (learned and acquired knowledge), entrepreneurial alliance (consortium, strategic alliance, and digital interface), society (social proximity, community needs, and social benefits), crowd contribution (collective intelligence, co-creation, and co-evolution), industry attractiveness (competition, entrepreneurial growth, and industrial revolution), and government support (public policies, regulations, and work practices) that help entrepreneurs to define governance, openness, action, and learning continuum (GOAL) through ESG coordination comprising environmental, social, and governance integration. These edges of the entrepreneurial prismatic structure necessarily help entrepreneurs in enhancing business and growth in the competitive environment. Innovations supported by crowd impetus through collective intelligence, co-creation, and co-evolution help entrepreneurs in seeding new product ideas in the utilitarian and hedonic market segments. Rapidly growing technologies are often attractive to embed innovations, but they need to be scrutinized for relative cost, time, risk, and derived value propositions. Consequently, these edges of marketing prism are sensitive to the PNS factors and resources within the industry and market ecosystems. Innovation, technology, and collective intelligence drive industry to a competitive dome and induce internal rivalry and competition among the firms to exploit existing opportunities and stay ahead of the leadership race (Rajagopal, 2024).

The elements of nine vertices include organizational culture and behavior of marketing firms, relationship management, interactive marketing, business canvas, marketing-mix sustainability, leadership, empowerment, and customer outreach. The vertices support any straight or angular structure in a construction with defined design. Likewise, the above vertices streamline the decision making, strategy development, and value creation processes in marketing despite the changing and disruptive influences. Besides the socialization of business by developing relationships and interactive transversalities across the consumer section, firms tend to strengthen their business foundations by building business canvas and marketing-mix block-by-block to gain market leadership. Empowering consumers and engaging them emotionally with the company in marketing activities help firms in narrowing their social proximity, generating social consciousness, and leveraging the geographic and ethnic outreach of consumers (Rajagopal, 2024).

In the rapidly changing market ecosystem today, entrepreneurs need a long sight to plan market outreach through convergence of social proximity with varied crowd attributes as illustrated in Fig. 2.2. Such convergence in entrepreneurial practices would help in developing strategic entrepreneurial vision towards successful market outreach. The market ecosystem is transforming from oligopolistic characteristics to segmented market pockets across geo-demographic segments. Accordingly, the conventional marketing practices are transforming to disruptive dynamics (futuristic propositions) and gradually overriding the contemporary marketing practices. The artificial intelligence (AI) and machine learning (ML) perspectives are driving new practices in marketing such as metaverse and disruptive marketing. The emerging market patterns are largely influenced by extrinsic attributes such as market competition, frugal innovations, technology, and convenience market practices (Pedroso et al., 2023). These factors significantly affect the industry attractiveness (new entrants, substitution effect, and bargaining power of suppliers and consumers), market demand, and supply situations. Consequently, entrepreneurs need to measure both longitudinal (temporal) and latitudinal (spatial) measures for successful market outreach through continuous learning, innovation, and process improvement.

The longitudinal outreach and latitudinal outreach have two principal domains comprising social proximity and mapping of crowd attributes. Entrepreneurs must identify social stakeholders based on co-created social values and spread of social benefits. They should exhibit openness towards social learning and bottom-up governance with focus on reverse accountability to translate collective actions into critical success factors. Social learning develops social empowerment among entrepreneurs over the family business entrepreneurial experience. Entrepreneurs can stay competitive by focusing on ethnic designs in congruence with the fashion trends in the market. However, to develop entrepreneurial competitiveness, entrepreneurs need to develop systematic resource mapping within the community infrastructure and public policy support in developing economies.

The pro entrepreneurship crowd attributes encourage social proximity under both longitudinal and latitudinal perspectives as explained in Fig. 2.2. Ensuring long-term relationship with external stakeholders in crowd domain helps not only to establish social networking but also to acquire new concepts and ideas through collective intelligence. Successful entrepreneurs analyze PNS factors and derive knowledge on new ideas,

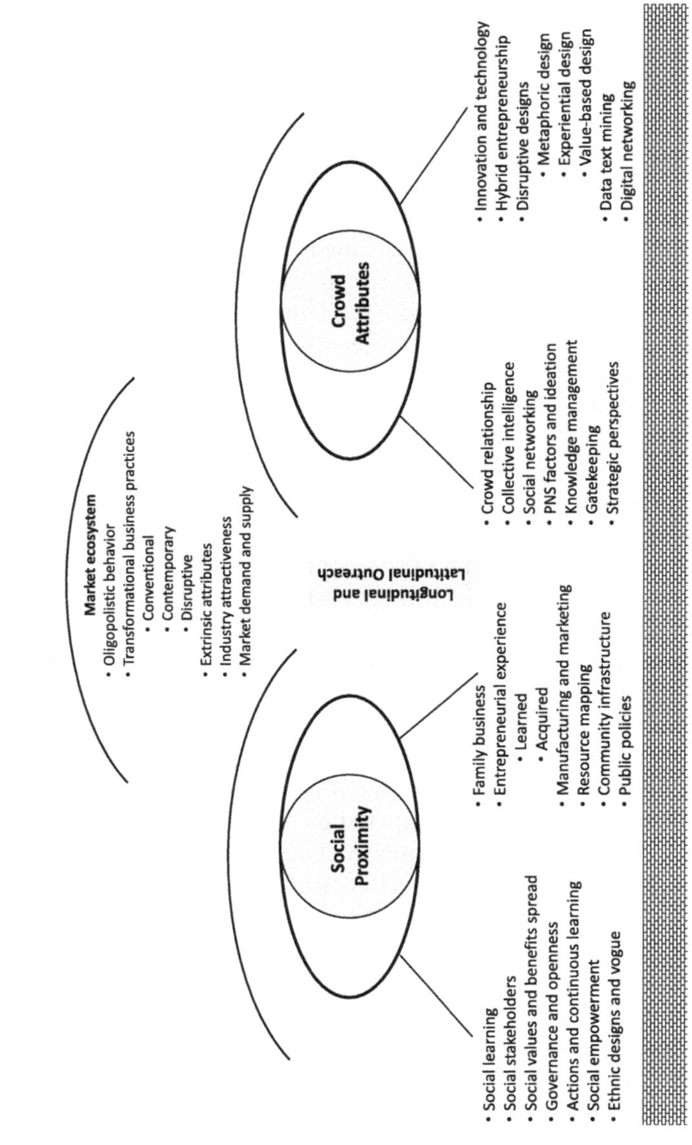

Fig. 2.2 Entrepreneurship, society, and proximity (*Source* Authors)

concepts, and strategic perspectives to perform entrepreneurial business and stay competitive in the marketplace. The crowd support and collective intelligence help in gatekeeping of rapidly changing technology, consumer preferences, fashion trends, and the nature of competition. The collective intelligence helps entrepreneurs in continuous learning about innovation and technology trends through data text mining and digital networking (Wu & Wu, 2023). Collective learning has become a part of social learning today, which encourages entrepreneurs to work with disruptive designs. Such design thinking in developing new entrepreneurial products can be explained to consumers metaphorically, driven by social values, and as an experiential output learned within the crowd environment.

Social proximity empowers entrepreneurs in both equity and equality perspectives across the entrepreneurial traits and demographic sections in a society, which help them to exercise equal control over their lifestyle, income resources, and employment. Empowering society holistically drives the members to take important decisions in routine activities and creates equal social and economic opportunities to support their lifestyle and socio-economic status. Empowering all sections of society equally ensures strong economic growth and social development in a region. On a collective level, social empowerment is implemented through public policies, corporate social responsibilities delivered by the corporations, public sector organizations, and social institutions, which help members of economically marginalized social communities. The social empowerment is aimed at improving the social and economic stature of marginalized communities including gender-based classes to improve their returns on assets, good health, education, social belonging, self-esteem, and self-confidence and develop economic opportunity. Holistically, social empowerment is developed across the four principal dimensions comprising psychological, organizational, economic, and cultural among the members of the community (Rajagopal, 2024).

Crowd-Based Business Modeling

Advances in information and communication technology have significantly increased harnessing the potential of social networking and developing interactive business models through collective intelligence and exploring possibilities of outsourcing business activities to the crowd of independent contributors. Innovative micro, small, and medium enterprises largely depend on social media in acquiring new ideas and stay competitive in the market. The new business models of the innovative enterprises are significantly supported by the external nexus of stakeholders, gatekeepers, and empathetic crowd in resolving business complexities and market challenges and creating superior value for the entrepreneurs. Therefore, building crowd capital is one of the changing perspectives in entrepreneurial business integrating both strategies and tactics to offer innovative propositions in business management (Täuscher, 2017). The contemporary entrepreneurial management is driven by aggregated wisdom of crowd to find solutions for rapidly increasing business challenges, which demand creation of value in business with logical framework and use of hybrid technology by exploiting the digital peer-to-peer platforms. Acquiring of entrepreneurial capabilities and competencies requires crowd interaction, which also helps in improving the inherent entrepreneurial practices through co-creation with crowd. The co-creation of innovative entrepreneurial products and services is benefited from crowd interaction, which generates collective intelligence towards the open access to resources and processes that could integrate micro tasks to create and deliver the end user products. The crowd interaction helps entrepreneurs to identify low-cost alternatives for frugal innovation and helps entrepreneurs in building effective business systems to use crowd-based contents and update the entrepreneurial practices (Kohler, 2015).

Crowdsourcing is an ideation process of sharing individual ideas, emotions, and experiences on business perspectives raging from business diplomacy to corporate strategies, and social marketing to customer value creation (Suvonova et al., 2019). It is an informal pool of information, which circulates in the society, spread across the social media channels and conventional word-of-mouth forums. The open innovation platforms and customer-centric innovations in a firm widely encourage crowdsourcing as a value-based tool to co-create community- and value-based business models. The crowdsourced information also guides manufacturing and business operations through the experiences of stakeholders, peers, gatekeepers, and consumers. Inspirational stimuli such as analogies are the prominent mechanism used to support designers (Goucher-Lambert & Cagan, 2019). Collective intelligence also helps the monitoring and evaluations of implementation and performance of crowd-based business models in companies. Collective intelligence also induces design-by-analogies and design-by-experience concepts, which helps in developing crowd-based business models (Moreno et al., 2014). Companies like

Google, Amazon, AT&T, Walmart, and Pitney Bowes have found a way to delve into the collective intelligence of their stakeholders and workforce and organize collective views categorically to improve the business performance of the firm (Rajagopal, 2021b).

The collective information repository serves as a source of open knowledge to the company, and at the same time, as a part of social movement to provide voice to customers to reach out companies. This is an outside-in inflow of information, which helps companies to understand the consumer perceptions, the trend of referrals, and styles of customer advocacy on products and services. Nonetheless, collective intelligence has open information feeds that require companies to employ robust information filters for quality output. Most customer-centric companies have developed their social media page on Facebook to enable the customers stay abreast with the new products and share opinion on the existing products and services. Crowdsourced information enables companies to learn about customer perceptions and emotions through shared experience and values, co-create products and services, and co-evolve with customers against competitors. In addition, text mining has also emerged as a tool to do research on user-generated contents across the Web and derive necessary output on key terms. Text mining has become a popular qualitative research tool to extract meaningful data available in text form. Text mining sources range from academic literature to social networking sites, posts and comments about the news, voice of the customer, speech-to-text data, and more tangible, digitally published documents (Rajagopal, 2021b). Digital networking in social interaction practices enhances the product ideation to develop new products. In addition, exploring new ideas by surfing on Internet has provided higher convenience to entrepreneurs than conventionally interacting on digital platforms within peers. The inquisitiveness in exploring new ideas on Internet has become convergent with scientific data text mining process by establishing criteria for the specific needs of innovation. The data text mining process provides diverse external influences within the entrepreneurial requirements and product—market ecosystem. Entrepreneurs gain insights through data text mining to innovate cost-effective and customer-centric product by earmarking competitive differentiators. The data text mining is largely supported by the development of open-source community, which enables entrepreneurs and innovators to collect data, analyze it, and use implications in innovation process.

The clustering of topics, sentiment taxonomy, and social network analysis are primarily used to analyze the text data obtained from the open sources on Internet. The open-source communities are refined crowds, which are engaged in knowledge sharing and production management, and stimulating market-driven innovative ideas to entrepreneurs. These communities also develop free software as public good in the interest of commons and stimulate entrepreneurship at the grassroots. The data text mining broadly helps entrepreneurs in strengthening creativity, identifying collaborators, and building low-cost business models by ensuring crowd support towards high performance and customer satisfaction (Hou et al., 2022).

Crowd creativity provides entrepreneurs with market-oriented and applied innovation perspectives. The collective intelligence acquired from digital networks and data text mining provides new opportunities to develop cost-effective working strategies based on user-generated contents to converge with PNS factors and value appreciations. However, such solutions largely remain untested and stand on hypothetical grounds, which poses risks in developing and implementing prima facie public strategies due to social and legal risks associated with the I-3-elements comprising impulsive ideation, situation interpretations, and infringement of intellectual property. Consequently, companies relying on the crowd-based business modeling need to explore possibility of digital rights management to stand clear on the intellectual property issues while prospecting the crowdsourcing of solutions (Rajagopal, 2021b). The crowd-based information needs to be validated against the risks of using intellectual property and strategic-fit on the business performance perspectives. Crowd commonly delivers raw information, which mitigates the risks associated with soliciting solutions on any uncommon or less occurring problem associated with the products and services. The unrefined crowd information is commonly proactive, premature, possessive, and persuasive, which needs to be judged within the social and business ecosystems (de Beer et al., 2017). The Internet and the open innovation have encouraged new ideas and solutions, which has made companies experience the longitudinal and latitudinal outreach in the consumer markets. Such ideas were based on developing products and services to provide consumer convenience, satisfaction, and enhance the business performance of firms. The main challenge faced in managing open innovation is measuring economic viability and technological feasibility accurately to enable the firms to take up innovation projects alongside the growing technology and develop convergence with the business model. Commonly, open innovations are low-priced and gain first mover advantage in the market; however, these products operate in a predetermined niche to survive the competition. Most companies focus on employing new technologies to serve customers with value, which not only delivers competitive advantage over the existing products in the market but is also able to create high perceived value.

Crowdsourcing is one of the principal ways of acquiring information via social networks, which leads to generating a pool of ideation, experience sharing, and finding solutions to the existing problems. Such categorical information repositories build collective intelligence over time, which is harnessed by the companies for developing customer-centric and crowd-based business models. Participants also conduct design advocacy for the fashion products, consumer electronics, food and health, home the, and other genre of public interest, which benefit customer-proactive companies to follow and fabricate. Intensive users on the social networks develop cognitive semantics by disseminating interconnected ideas and thoughts, of which thought leadership is built on the networks, and opinions gradually polarize to some flagship ideas (Rajagopal, 2021b).

Social network analytics is an advanced digital data analysis perspective applied to disruptive innovation and radical entrepreneurship concepts, which engages in the fields of public health, information spreading, sustainability, and consumer electronics innovation. Entrepreneurs benefit to acquire real-time perspectives from data text mining. The clustering of ideas, market potentials, sentiment classifications, and new market-led lexicons are obtained through data text mining, which enables entrepreneurs to develop competitive performance and ensure long-term business growth. Social media has widened the opportunities for consumer-oriented firms to expand their market beyond the brick-and-mortar stores. Consumer networks are used by most firms to supplement the traditional sources of buyer insights with a wealth of information gathered by listening in to community sites such as Facebook, LinkedIn, and Twitter, and customer forums and product review services. Monitoring the information flow on social media gives firms a unique access to unfiltered feedback from customers, which may not be possible to obtain through other means such as focus groups and surveys. Firms intending to experiment with monitoring the Web can outsource the entire process to third parties, or build the capabilities internally (Rajagopal, 2021b).

MIC Factors

Entrepreneurship today is influenced by the MIC factors comprising market consciousness, innovation perspectives, and consumer value creation. The social consciousness towards crowd behavior to acquire collective intelligence also significantly contributes to the market-oriented entrepreneurship in developing economies. Broadly these factors catalyze transforming the level of innovation in response to the changing consumption culture and utilitarian values associated with the entrepreneurial products and services. Therefore, the social dynamics driven by the collective intelligence largely contribute to the changes in social lifestyle and values (Strupeit & Palm, 2016). The micro, small, and medium enterprises gain competitive advantage in the marketplace by developing strategic approaches that are congruent with the consumer consciousness and collective intelligence. These enterprises stay competitive in the marketplace by adapting to the crowd-based entrepreneurial decisions over the conventional practices. The crowd-based design thinking helps micro, small, and medium enterprises to connect to the urban economic geo-demographics beyond niche markets, which creates chain effects in developing consumer awareness about entrepreneurial innovative products, disseminates consumer advocacy towards innovative consumption patterns, and derives macro entrepreneurial effects in urban markets. Connecting local enterprises with urban markets, entrepreneurs reinforce competitive differentiators, which enable stakeholders and consumers to realize the social values and inculcate loyalty towards entrepreneurial products and services. The market consciousness among entrepreneurial products is widely supported by the information and technology-led digital platforms, enabling successful social networking and human interface with social media. The interactive innovation platforms generate awareness among stakeholders and consumers on the evolution of innovative products and stimulate varied value propositions on the types of innovation carried out on open platforms. The views of customers, stakeholders, and market players on the innovative products of micro, small, and medium enterprises enhance the scope of marketability of these products, scale and size of enterprise, and the collective growth of firms beyond niche market. The local enterprises, which acquire the knowledge and skills through collective intelligence, override the conventional competencies and rise in the market by the sheer dint of crowd cognition and organizational compatibility with contemporary markets.

The social consciousness, social identity, and market consciousness are thematically congruent in customer-centric business competition (Sting et al., 2019).

Social enterprises are community-conscious organizations while commercial enterprises at the local level are socially conscious firms. Therefore, entrepreneurial consciousness towards society and market is evenly distributed across entrepreneurial operations. Market consciousness helps entrepreneurs to develop co-created solutions for predetermined social needs embedded in PNS factors. Market conscious enterprises irrespective of their scale of operation and size (micro, small, and medium enterprises) evolve within the business canvas focusing on the key activities, key partners, key resources, value propositions, customer relationships, customer segments, channels, cost structures, and revenue streams. The entrepreneurial marketing approach involves cost-effective activities by avoiding formal market research or involving mass promotions strategies to promote business. However, entrepreneurs of small and medium business segments significantly depend on their personal networks to collect information about consumers and the market. These entrepreneurs heavily use consumer psychodynamics and the inter-personal communication such as word-of mouth to promote their products and services (Copley, 2013). Micro, small, and medium enterprises, which are conscious to market dynamics, co-create business models with collective intelligence and stakeholder preferences to mark differentiation and gain competitive advantage. In addition, value-conscious consumers demand cost innovative pricing approaches in the mass markets in both developed and emerging markets. Competitive consumer products companies, therefore, enter alliances with emerging Chinese companies to gain cost innovation capabilities and deliver high customer value (Rajagopal, 2021b; Williamson & Zeng, 2009).

As the market consciousness grows, the entrepreneurial innovation compatible to consumer preferences increases to enable consumers to experience self-actualization and self-esteem on products of cultural and ethnic values. Further, the competitive strategies, frugal innovations, and stakeholder engagement contribute to develop differentiation among competing products and gain competitive advantage. Over the changing state of market behavior, most entrepreneurs stay skeptical about the market share and predicted profits. However, ethnic brands enjoy the benefits of fashion trends and social consciousness, and stay as referrals to diffuse consumer experiences, values, and contemporary vision on the changing consumer preferences. A careful analysis of a microenvironment indicates whether a company can successfully enter a specific market. It may be hypothesized that prosperity of a nation depends on the productivity with which it uses its human, capital, and natural resources. This is manifested in the way a nation's firms compete. Productivity, in turn, is a function of the interplay of many factors including political, legal, and macroeconomic context; the quality of the microeconomic business environment; and the sophistication of company operations and strategy. Low-priced products and crowdfunding have proved to be a worthy combination in the niche market evolved around price conscious, gender-based, and millennial consumers segment (Rajagopal, 2022). Most customer-centric enterprises develop new products as 'design-to-market' by involving consumers in co-creation process. Such consumer and stakeholder engagements in new product development help enterprises to effectively manage market trends and develop sustainable consumer attitude and consumption behavior. Therefore, it is observed that value-oriented consumer behavior and consumer value chain support entrepreneurship with market consciousness.

Business operations of micro, small, and medium enterprises are significantly influenced by both tangible and intangible factors comprising market consciousness among entrepreneurs, innovative perspectives within enterprises, and creation of consumer value as exhibited in Fig. 2.3. Entrepreneurs acquire contemporary market information through collective intelligence and by observing through the crowd behavior. These factors influence socio-psychological emotions of entrepreneurs towards generating market consciousness, which helps in determining the differentiators of products and services to develop market competitiveness. The conventional human interface has been transformed to digital social networking, which allows both spatial and temporal interactions to understand the contemporary market behavior. These factors constitute the social side of market consciousness. Scientific proposition in developing design-to-market strategies, most enterprises tend to develop the collaborative business canvas with internal and external stakeholders. Besides market consciousness, various innovation perspectives also affect the entrepreneur-market interface. Among the broad taxonomy of entrepreneurial innovation, the open innovation, which is largely supported by the crowed behavior and collective intelligence, evolves frugal innovation with embedded utilitarian values through co-creation and strategic alliances with society and industry (Karami &

Read, 2021). Successful innovations emerging from the micro, small, and medium enterprises are led by CVI considerations encompassing cost consciousness, value appreciation, and innovation lifecycle. The open and frugal innovations are largely supported by effective internal and external stakeholder engagement, which ensures minimizing cost, time, and risk factors while optimizing consumption, benefits, and profit perspectives. Market orientation of frugal innovations developed by micro, small, and medium enterprises can be strengthened through SVL synchronization comprising servitization, value-for-money, and driving loyalty through repeat buying process. These enterprises need to emphasize on AATAR factors which require creating *awareness* about *attributes* of innovation, exhibiting innovating products for *trial*, and ensuring *availability* in local markets to drive the *repeat buying* behavior among consumers.

Entrepreneurs can attain higher market consciousness to ensure effective market interface by analyzing the available information to identify the right market segment and reliable influencer appeal to develop applied enthusiasm (beyond emotional perspectives) as illustrated in Fig. 2.3. Entrepreneurs can conduct self-appraisal to evaluate market consciousness and market interface. The innovative perspectives are also connected with entrepreneur-market interface, which helps in exploring new opportunities, applied design thinking, experimenting new ideas, and leveraging community resources by reviewing the possible uncertainties in developing new entrepreneurial business models (Tantawy et al., 2021). Integrating market consciousness and market interface in the entrepreneurial process helps entrepreneurs in creating consumer value across urban geo-demographic segments through emotional intelligence and transformational consumption culture. Therefore, entrepreneurs need to invest in creating consumer consciousness through consumer advocacy, which would self-propagate through consumer psychodynamics based on the quality of consumer experience. Consumer value can be created within the learned (social and conventional), acquired (market-based and fashion trends), and interrelated (self-actualization and self-esteem) value systems.

The successful execution of MIC factors-based entrepreneurial strategy reinforces entrepreneurial bond among innovation, value creation, and market interface (Grönroos et al., 2015). Such bonding leads to nurturing of entrepreneurial emotions and economic compatibility of entrepreneurial trade with the identified markets to serve varied taxonomy of business (business-to-consumer, business-to-business, consumer-to-consumer, and online-to-offline market segments) today. However, in

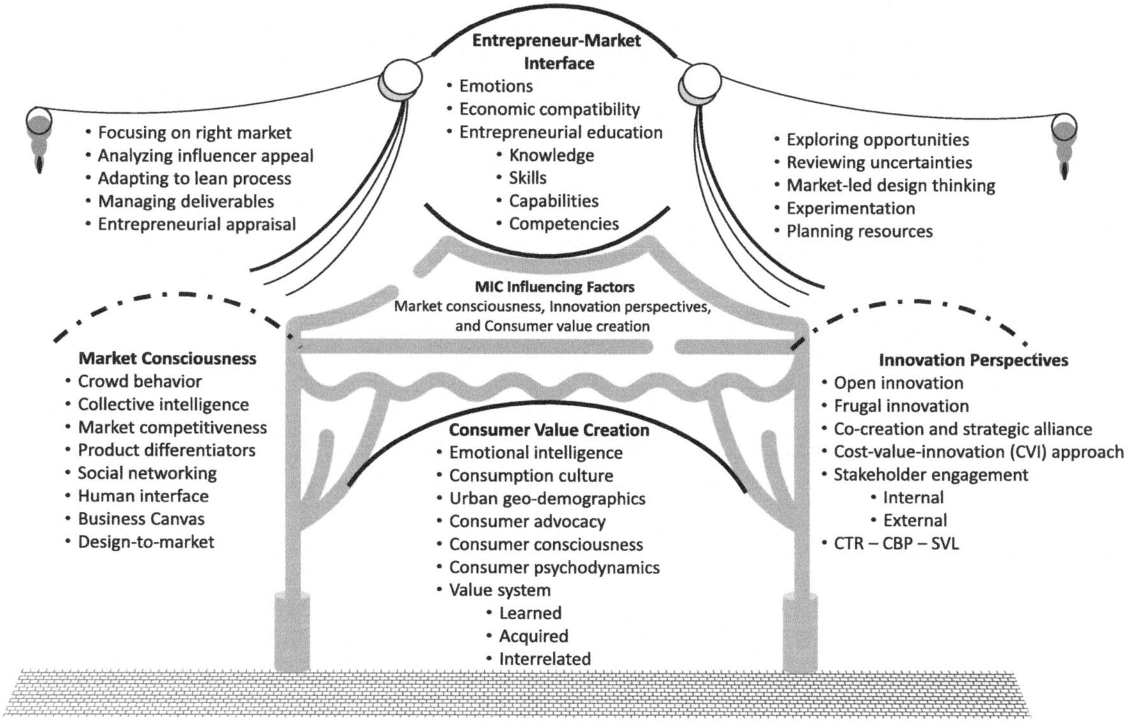

Fig. 2.3 Experiencing entrepreneur market interface (*Source* Authors)

this process, the concern for entrepreneurial education (He et al., 2024) is always atop, which helps in acquiring and disseminating knowledge, technology-based entrepreneurial skills, and competencies as explained in Fig. 2.3.

Changing innovation perspectives in both urban and rural markets are oriented towards product attributes, product lifecycle, and value for money. These indicators are knitted around the price perspectives of utilitarian value of innovative entrepreneurial products. Therefore, micro, small, and medium enterprises are consciously focusing on reducing the CTR factors to increase the consumption, benefits, and profit (CBP) factors of innovative products. These factors encourage entrepreneurs to develop low-cost, acceptable value, and long lifecycle products that are affordable by the consumers and encourage potential for repeat buying. Strategic thinking helps new entrants to adjust ecosystem with the socio-economic, cultural, and market-led factors that influence one another and stimulate the management of the design cube comprising design-to-market, design-to-society, and design-to-value. The business ecosystem is fundamentally based on these triadic design pillars. Large companies tend to explore radically new technology to disrupt existing markets, while the new entrants focus on pursuing value-adding improvement in the existing products and technologies on the frugal innovation platform. In this process of orchestrating business ecosystems, multinational companies and joint ventures follow an integrative and long-term perspectives in business embedding business goals and strategic interests in decision making (Rajagopal, 2021c). In the competitive business environment, large firms operate with open ecosystems to gain competitive leverage by commercializing open-innovation and reverse-innovation products. This strategy helps firms in delivering high customer value and inculcate perceptions among customers on collective creativity. Consequently, firms can retain the loyalty and support of ecosystem partners and stakeholders to ensure their continued performance in the marketplace. Continuous learning and exploring ways to catch-up with changes in the industry drive firms to stay agile with the dynamic business ecosystems. Such strategic business goals help these firms develop backward and forward linkages with suppliers and buyer-groups to develop operational integration (Zahra & Nambisan, 2012).

It is often challenging for the small companies to adapt to a structural business model over the traditional family-based organizational structure. Such business confinement needs small firms in emerging markets to co-evolve with large firms and catch-up with them to improve the manufacturing and marketing processes, and the productivity rather than engaging in frugal innovations for niche markets. Continuous growth in innovation and technologies is the principal stimulant for companies to gain competitive differentiation and leadership in the global markets and gain high brand equity to drive consumers towards new buying preferences and exploring new market segments (Rajagopal, 2021c). However, it is often hard for consumers to adopt innovations, gain confidence in deriving values appropriately, and derive competitive advantages from the innovative offerings over the existing and predetermined products and services. Companies growing in a competitive marketplace monitor both new and incremental innovations to explore their influence on firms' survival and growth. In addition, the market orientation, firm's size, its international dimension, and age of the business leader at entry are the control variables most influential on survival (Ortiz-Villajos & Sotoca, 2018; Rajagopal, 2021c).

The values of internal (leader and employees) and external (investors and consumers) stakeholders are embedded in the market ecosystem of micro, small, and medium enterprises, which is founded on the culture, ethnicity, and collective intelligence. The applied entrepreneurial thinking, which stimulates market competitiveness encompassing social values is based on the PNS and CBP factors. Consequently, market-oriented value system emerges out of the social and economic indicators, which affects businesses and their performance with purpose. The taxonomy of market-oriented value system encapsulates learned, acquired, and interrelated consumer values across geo-demographic segments. Customers acquire values from strong external market influences and experience sharing among fellow customers. Commonly acquired values play temporary stimulus among customers towards buying. It takes a long time for companies to establish the acquired values as the drivers of decision among customers. Experience sharing, internal motivation, and external influence constitute the key elements in forming the acquired values among customers. The 4Es comprising emotions, economic complementarity, education and undated knowledge, and experimental behavior inculcate interrelated values among consumers towards their association with relevant products and services. Exploring interrelated values helps firms analyze the suitability of launching new products and brand extensions in the new or existing consumer segments. The value incentives encourage social value-led firms to develop syncretic stewardship, which drives firms on socialization of business through corporate social responsibility programs (Rajagopal, 2021c).

The crowd-based business models with collective intelligence and commitment of stakeholders significantly affect the value propositions of consumers. The micro, small, and medium enterprises tend to create value and delivery products and services through effective entrepreneurial social responsibility. These perspectives are moderated by the crowd behavior, collective intelligence, consumption, and constituents of market ecosystem. These enterprises co-create value on digital platforms through global–local interactive information exchange. However, micro, small, and medium enterprises need to rethink on modular designs and co-creation of business models within global–local business dynamics (Bridgens et al., 2017). Broadly, the consumer value creation is derived through conscious cognition, actions in subconscious mind, unconscious perceptions, and materialistic reasoning. The cognitive ergonomics of customers (emotions, perceptions, and memories and storyboards), knowledge, beliefs, and trust and the abilities of information analysis constitute the conscious cognition, which embeds customer value perceptions. Customer values are also affected by unaffordable desires, social comparisons triggering inferiority feelings, and the need for socio-economic equity. These attributes evolve in the subconscious mind of customers, while the value destructions and transitions occur unconsciously in the minds of customers. Periodical assessment of customer value being intangible and transitionary, enterprises tend to develop agile marketing strategies to stimulate local and regional business growth. Enterprises adapting to design-to-value concepts tend to put customers first in developing and implementing pro-customer marketing strategies comprising push (resource-based marketing approach with all elements of marketing-mix) and pull (psychodynamics and non-zero-sum game) strategies. Customer value-centric companies usually engage in knowing (exploring value perceptions), doing (implementing pro-customer strategies), and being (enjoying the state of win-win by serving the customers), which enables them to achieve performance with purpose (Rajagopal, 2021c).

References

Ano, B., & Bent, R. (2022). Human determinants influencing the digital transformation strategy of multigenerational family businesses: A multiple-case study of five French growth-oriented family firms. *Journal of Family Business Management, 12*(4), 876–891.

Aparicio, S., Urbano, D., & Audretsch, D. (2016). Institutional factors, opportunity entrepreneurship and economic growth: Panel data evidence. Technological Forecasting and Social Change, *102*, 45–61. https://doi.org/10.1016/j.techfore.2015.04.006

Bridgens, B., Hobson, K., Lilley, D., Lee, J., Scott, J. L., & Wilson, G. T. (2017). Closing the loop on e-waste: A multidisciplinary perspective. *Journal of Industrial Ecology, 39*(1), 1–13.

Chou, D. C. (2018). Applying design thinking method to social entrepreneurship project. *Computer Standards & Interfaces, 55*, 73–79.

Copley, P. (2013). The need to deliver higher-order skills in the context of marketing in SMEs. *Industry and Higher Education, 27*(6), 465–476.

de Beer, J., McCarthy, I. P., Soliman, A., & Treen, E. (2017). Click here to agree: Managing intellectual property when crowdsourcing solutions. *Business Horizons, 60*(2), 207–217.

Garvin, D. A., & Levesque, L. C. (2006). Meeting challenges of the corporate entrepreneurship. *Harvard Business Review, 84*(10), 102–110.

Grönroos, C., Strandvik, T., and Heinonen, K. (2015). Value Co-creation: Critical reflections service marketing and management for the future. *The Nordic School*, 69–81.

Goucher-Lambert, K., & Cagan, J. (2019). Crowdsourcing inspiration: Using crowd generated inspirational stimuli to support designer ideation. *Design Studies, 61*(1), 1–29.

He, L., Zheng, L. J., Sharma, P., & Leung, T. Y. (2024). Entrepreneurship education and established business activities: An international perspective. *The International Journal of Management Education*, 22(1), https://doi.org/10.1016/j.ijme.2023.100922.

Hyytinen, A. (2021). Shared problem solving and design thinking in entrepreneurship research. *Journal of Business Venturing Insights*, 16. https://doi.org/10.1016/j.jbvi.2021.e00254

Hou, S., Zhang, X., Yi, B., & Tang, Y. (2022). Public attitudes on open source communities in China: A text mining analysis. *Technology in Society*, 71. https://doi.org/10.1016/j.techsoc.2022.102112

Jaradat, R. M., Keating, C. B., & Bradley, J. M. (2017). Individual capacity and organizational competency for systems thinking. *IEEE Systems Journal, 12*(2), 1203–1210.

Judge, W. Q. (2011). *Organizational capacity for change dimension 5: Systems thinking*. Business Expert Press.

Kapasi, I., & Rosli, A. (2020). The practice of "we": A framework for balancing rigour and relevance in entrepreneurship scholarship. *Journal of Business Venturing Insights, 14*. https://doi.org/10.1016/j.jbvi.2020.e00202

Karami, M., & Read, S. (2021). Co-creative entrepreneurship. *Journal of Business Venturing, 36*(4).https://doi.org/10.1016/j.jbusvent.2021.106125

Kohler, T. (2015). Crowdsourcing-based business models: How to create and capture value. *California Management Review, 57*(4), 63–84.

Lee, Y. S., & Eesley, C. (2018). The persistence of entrepreneurship and innovative immigrants. *Research Policy, 47*(6), 1032–1044.

Mingjie, L., Qiaohong, C., Qi, S., & Yubo, J. (2020). Hybrid neural network for Sina Weibo sentiment analysis. *IEEE Transactions on Computational Social Systems, 7*(4), 983–990.

Moreno, D. P., Hernández, A. A., Yang, M. C., Otto, K. N., Hölttä-Otto, K., & Linsey, J. S. (2014). Fundamental studies in design-by-analogy: A focus on domain-knowledge experts and applications to transactional design problems. *Design Studies, 35*(3), 232–272.

Ortiz-Villajos, J. M., & Sotoca, S. (2018). Innovation and business survival: A long-term approach. *Research Policy, 47*(8), 1418–1436.

Parente, R., El Tarabishy, A., Vesci, M., & Botti, A. (2018). The epistemology of humane entrepreneurship: Theory and proposal for future research agenda. *Journal of Small Business Management, 56*, 30–52.

Pedroso, I. D., Soares, M.A.F., de Aguiar Dutra, A. R., Cubas, A. L. V., de Andrade Guerra J. B. S. O., & Brem, A. (2023). Frugal innovation development for sustainability: The case of extractivism of the "Butia catarinensis" in Brazil. *Journal of Cleaner Production*, 412. https://doi.org/10.1016/j.jclepro.2023.137318

Porfírio, J. A., Carrilho, T., & Mónico, L. S. (2016). Entrepreneurship in different contexts in cultural and creative industries. *Journal of Business Research, 69*(11), 5117–5123.

Rajagopal. (2021a). *The business design cube: Converging markets, society, and customer values to grow competitive in business*. Business Expert Press.

Rajagopal. (2021b). *Crowd-based business models—Using collective intelligence for market competitiveness*. Palgrave Macmillan.

Rajagopal (2021c). *Crowd-Based Business Models—Using collective intelligence for market competitiveness*. Palgrave Macmillan.

Rajagopal. (2022). *Agile marketing strategies—New approaches to engaging consumer behavior*. Springer.

Rajagopal. (2024). *Proximity marketing: Converging community, consciousness, and consumption*. Business Expert Press.

Reeves, M., Haanaes, K., & Sinha, J. (2015). Navigating the dozens of different strategy options. *Harvard Business Review, 93*(6), 1–17.

Sting, F. J., Fuchs, C., Schlickel, M., & Alexy, O. (2019). *How to Overcome the Bias We Have Toward Our Own Ideas*. Harvard Business School Press.

Strupeit, L., & Palm, A. (2016). Overcoming barriers to renewable energy diffusion: Business models for customer-sited solar photovoltaics in Japan, Germany and the United States. *Journal of Cleaner Production, 123*, 124–136.

Suvonova, H., Lee, J. Y., & Park, T. (2019). Organizational preparedness for corporate entrepreneurship and psychological capital: Does the managerial level matter? *Asian Journal of Technology Innovation, 27*(3), 359–376.

Tantawy, M., Herbert, K., McNally, J. J., Mengel, T., Piperopoulos, P., & Foord, D. (2021). Bringing creativity back to entrepreneurship education: Creative self-efficacy, creative process engagement, and entrepreneurial intentions. *Journal of Business Venturing Insights*, 15. https://doi.org/10.1016/j.jbvi.2021.e00239

Täuscher, K. (2017). Leveraging collective intelligence: How to design and manage crowd-based business models. *Business Horizons, 60*(2), 237–245.

Tazzit, S., Jing, L., Ma, J., & Jaradat, R. (2023). Systems-thinking skills preferences evaluation model of practitioners using hybrid weight determination and extended VIKOR model under COVID-19. *Advanced Engineering Informatics*, 57. https://doi.org/10.1016/j.aei.2023.102107

Wiklund, J., Wright, M., & Zahra, S. A. (2019). Conquering relevance: Entrepreneurship research's grand challenge. *Entrepreneurship Theory and Practice, 43*(3), 419–436.

Williamson, P. J., & Zeng, M. (2009). Value-for-money strategies for recessionary times. *Harvard Business Review, 87*(3), 66–74.

Wu, J., & Wu, L. (2023). Impacts of digital inclusive finance on household entrepreneurship. *Finance Research Letters*, 56. https://doi.org/10.1016/j.frl.2023.104114

Zahra, S. A., & Nambisan, S. (2012). Entrepreneurship and strategic thinking in business ecosystems. *Business Horizons, 55*(3), 219–229.

Zheng, W., Yang, B., & McLean, G. N. (2010). Linking organizational culture, structure, strategy, and organizational effectiveness: Mediating role of knowledge management. *Journal of Business Research, 63*(7), 763–771.

PART II

Planning the Transformation

CHAPTER 3

The Game Analytics

Abstract This chapter discusses the prelude to these models through the convergence of divergent factors of the game analytics. The PNS factors, increasing crowd influence, and socio-economic factors have been discussed in the book as the game foundation, which broadly deliberates R3 analytics comprising entrepreneurial attributes on resilience, returns, and risks. The transformational elements comprising technology, market, human elements, and organizational attributes in the context of local and global entrepreneurial environment have been discussed in this chapter. This chapter has discussed comprehensively the entrepreneurial transformation as a foundational attribute, which contributes to critical success of the firm and ensures long-term competitive success. The discussions also explore the role of government in supporting entrepreneurial transformation by resolving the visible and invisible challenges embedded in local firms (e.g., Liu & Lee, 2019). The crowd-based ideation, entrepreneurial blueprint, conceptualization, and decision making are critically examined in this chapter, which leads to discussion of ground-breaking concepts on the three-dimensional organizational square comprising organizational design, decision making, change management, and strategies and tactics.

Keywords Entrepreneurial transformation · Resilience · Returns · Risks · Change management

Rajagopal and A. Rajagopal, *Unmasking Invisible Challenges in Entrepreneurship*, Palgrave Studies of Entrepreneurship and Social Challenges in Developing Economies,
https://doi.org/10.1007/978-3-031-63653-0_3

As the game changer models constitute the core of discussion of this book, this chapter discusses the prelude to these models through the convergence of divergent factors of the game analytics. PNS factors, increasing crowd influence, and socio-economic factors have been discussed in the book as the game foundation, which broadly deliberates R3 analytics. The crowd-based ideation, entrepreneurial blueprint, conceptualization, and decision making are critically examined in this chapter, which leads to discussion of ground-breaking concepts on the three-dimensional organizational square comprising organizational design, decision making, change management, and strategies and tactics.

The Transformational Elements

Market orientation of entrepreneurial ventures and technological advancements has made significant contributions to the development of entrepreneurial business across different scales of business and territorial setups. The use of advanced technological tools and techniques in developing products at micro, small, and medium enterprises has revolutionized market-oriented innovations supported by the crowd behavior, collective intelligence, and value-driven economic transactions. The crowd-based innovations are synchronized through block chain process expanding their proximity through local partners and digital networking (Jiang & Zheng, 2021). Entrepreneurs are now being targeted by the large firms and consumers encouraging to co-create and get actively engaged in the open innovation process. Besides innovation and technology, the community infrastructure provided by the local government encourages entrepreneurs to develop collective design thinking and process mapping for innovative products. The public policies in developing economies have been serving as the backbone by providing access to the technology at low cost and develop workplace ergonomics to facilitate innovation at the local level. Among many game changer factors, developing conducive entrepreneurial ecosystem converges with the market requirements which play a significant role in the local area innovation and technology co-creation (Schleicher et al., 2016). Therefore, governments in developing economies have invested enormously in developing local area technology and innovation for transformation of entrepreneurship and its ubiquitous development. The green entrepreneurship is also evolving as one of the transformational drivers in support of green economy and changing consumer preferences towards sustainable innovation. These factors have shown significant increase in both product availability and user preferences in view of environmental concerns leveraging new entrepreneurial opportunities.

The entrepreneurial collaborations between small and large enterprises with focus on technology-led growth are largely driven by the profit motivation in both local and urban enterprise scaling. Consequently, the enterprise governance requires critical intervention of internal and external stakeholders. The growth and acceleration of local enterprises today depend on the co-evolution model contributed by both small and large enterprises embedding inclusivity and diversity in practice. On social and humanistic perspectives, the entrepreneurial transformation has been observed on gender-based entrepreneurial initiatives that help in restructuring the growth acceleration and accountability in entrepreneurship (Kayes et al., 2005). These factors of entrepreneurial transformation have exhibited efficiency, effectiveness, and entrepreneurial architecture in various types of industrial segment such as transportation, public health, consumer electronics, artificial intelligence (AI), and machine learning (ML), which typically contributes to the collective and co-creative growth of the enterprises. In addition, applied entrepreneurial education has prolifically contributed new skills among potential entrepreneurs. The systematic and crowd knowledge (fuzzy learning model) helps entrepreneurs in developing innovative business mindset and fosters experiential learning space to offer competitive products and services (La Guardia et al., 2014). The entrepreneurial transformation is affected by various interrelated economic, managerial, and geographic attributes, which have been exhibited in Fig. 3.1.

Entrepreneurial transformation is largely governed by the existing ecosystem and the dynamic attributes therein act as game changers for most micro, small, and medium enterprises as exhibited in Fig. 3.1. Entrepreneurial ecosystem comprising major elements includes public policies on micro, small, and medium enterprises to provide financial support and develop human capital by imparting knowledge on market trends, technology, and skills. Entrepreneurship-oriented public policies help these enterprises to evolve innovation and design thinking out of existing culture and ethnicity using community infrastructure besides individual firm amenities. The entrepreneurial ecosystems also constitute their different layers of market taxonomy, which can be explained as pyramidal transition from the grassroots (bottom-of-the-pyramid) to the *big middle* (upper, average, and lower mass consumer segment) and to the

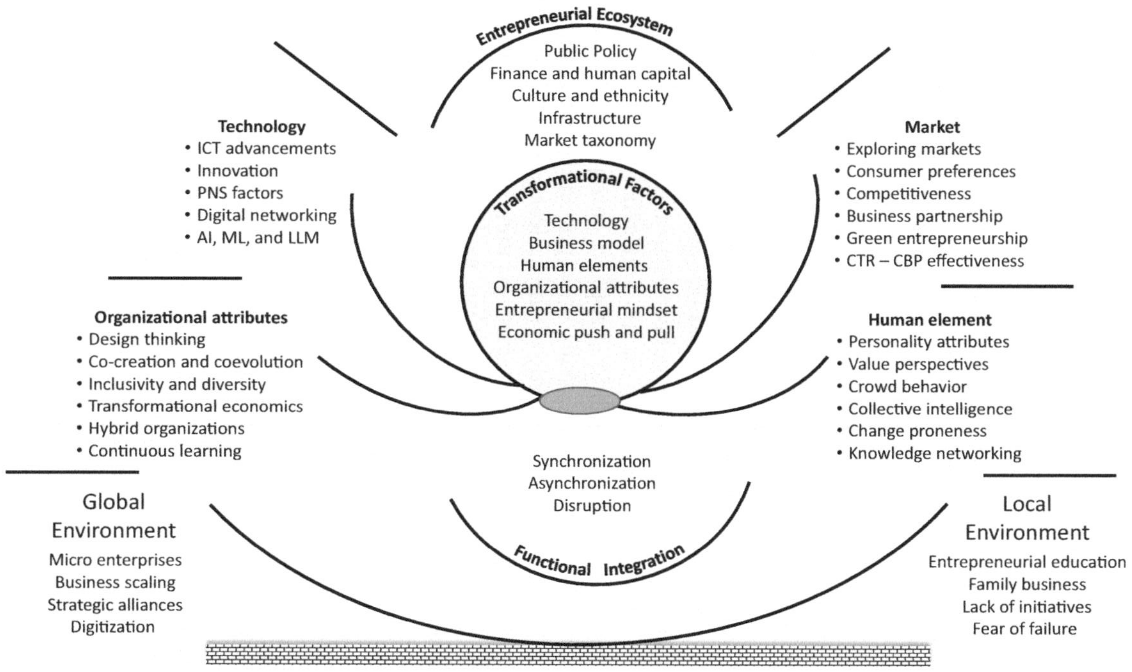

Fig. 3.1 Elements influencing entrepreneurial transformation (*Source* Authors)

premium consumer segment. Largely, these enterprises are founded at the bottom-of-the-pyramid, which struggles continuously to explore business passage to penetrate higher layers of market. The transformational factors are embedded in the entrepreneurial ecosystem, which need to be categorically explored to successfully transform these enterprises. The emerging challenges in transforming micro, small, and medium enterprises are to develop compatibility with rapidly changing technology driven by artificial intelligence and machine learning. In this process, enterprises need to acquire knowledge and skills to develop new business models integrating business-to-business (B-to-B), business-to-consumer (B-to-C), consumer-to-consumer (C-to-C), and online-to-offline (O-to-O). In transforming enterprises, one of the most sensitive perspectives is to guide entrepreneurial mindset within existing organizational culture and the attributes of human elements. These are intangible factors influenced by personality, cognition, emotions, and self-actualization to determine the need for transformation and accepting the challenges in the change management process. However, economic push (competitive returns) and pull (knowledge and desire) factors subjectively support the entrepreneurs in transforming conventional firms to contemporary standards and stay competitive in the marketplace as explained in Fig. 3.1. Entrepreneurial ecosystem in driving transformational factors needs a systematic functional integration, which is often an uphill task. Synchronizing functional integration is a linear process, which requires to be streamlined with the personality of entrepreneurs, available resources, technology, and public policy support while asynchronization process embeds applied perspectives by analyzing cause and effect, trial and error, and cost and risk matrices. Nonetheless, transformational factors are also affected by the disruptive design thinking, disruptive business models, and disruptive value creation.

Technology and market behavior are the dynamic factors in transforming entrepreneurial business. The advancements in information and communication technology have significantly influenced entrepreneurs to explore PNS factors and designing of low-cost and value-based innovation through digital networking. In addition, the increasing role of artificial intelligence and machine learning in designing and manufacturing market-driven products has given new impetus to entrepreneurs to stay competitive in the marketplace by providing customer-centric products of contemporary fashion. Also, there is an increasing trend of large language models (LLM), which support deep learning models for artificial intelligence based on large datasets. These models are known as underlying transformers, which support AI and ML neural networks to uplift the entrepreneurial performance within the changing technology ecosystem. Such technology-led transformation motivates entrepreneurs to explore new markets and consumer segments to match with their preferences and stay competitive in the marketplace. To manage entrepreneurial transformation and ensure entrepreneurial business performance, it becomes necessary to develop business partnerships and strategic alliances to share CTR factors and CBP outcomes. The combination of technology and market factors can be explained in the context of PESTO model comprising *performance* effectiveness, entrepreneurial *earning*, *sharing* profit with partners, managing productivity-based *transformation*, and developing cost-effective *operational* efficiency. The PESTO model is associated with the collaborative entrepreneurship, which recommends strategic alliances and governance partnership. The long-run impact of PESTO model of entrepreneurship is reinforced through EATE factors consisting of *expertise*, *accountability*, *trust* in partnership, and *experience* derived from the collaborative entrepreneurship.

Human elements in constituting organizational culture have underlying effect in nurturing micro, small, and medium enterprises. The internal and external stakeholders and crowd advocacy through collective intelligence sensibly guide open design thinking process, which leads to co-creation and co-evolution of customer-centric innovations in products and services. Such knowledge management practices help in promoting continuous learning and developing new insights on transformational economics, which guide the entrepreneurial journey to a new level crossing over the conventional wisdom. The inclusivity and diversity contribute to the contemporary value perspectives, which reinforce change proneness among the internal and external stakeholders and encourage knowledge networking within the entrepreneurial ecosystem. A combined effect of technology, market behavior, human elements, and organizational attributes develops functional integration and in a synchronized manner transform the existing entrepreneurial ecosystem to bridge the global–local entrepreneurial environment. Consequently, entrepreneurs learn from global scenarios, the scaling of business through strategic alliances and digitization in micro enterprises. Such visualization and experience stimulate entrepreneurial education at local level to overcome the fear of failure on new initiatives. The symbiosis between global and local entrepreneurial ecosystem not only motivates individual entrepreneurs but also strengthens the family business culture.

Previous studies suggest that there are significant cross-sectional and longitudinal variations in the entrepreneurial practices across the different sizes of enterprises at local and regional level, which affects the social and economic characteristics of entrepreneurs. Often, entrepreneurs express that transformational process of entrepreneurial activities have high impact on cost, time, and risk (CTR) factors, which restrict change proneness among entrepreneurs and lead to instable entrepreneurial business. Though several frameworks have been developed across developing economies, it is required that governments and corporate sector must ensure risk protection approaches to grow local enterprises as a transformational economic agent (Graham & Bonner, 2024). In this process, the local enterprises must be capable of conducting advanced entrepreneurial activities by obtaining the market externalities with the capabilities to absorb risk and exploit latent market opportunities. However, this argument is less common presuming that entrepreneurs in local economic setup are innately weak. Therefore, one of the major challenges in transforming entrepreneurial culture is to revamp entrepreneurial knowledge and skills for social entrepreneurship with focus on gender perspectives (Bae et al., 2014). Conventionally, social enterprises are considered as hybrid organizations perusing innovation, technology, and value-driven products with a social purpose. This justifies that entrepreneurs possess intrinsic cognition to grow with societal changes and survive to the best existence fit. These transformational factors have both implicit and explicit impacts on entrepreneurial transformation to provide competitive advantage in the marketplace. The transformational mindset of entrepreneurs must be explained as unique opportunity by reducing cognitive biases and raising confidence among entrepreneurs to manage the new generation enterprises (Buratti et al., 2022). The contemporary technological drive with AI and ML can transform entrepreneurial practices and provide global accessibility to entrepreneurial markets within the cyberspace environment.

R3—Resilience, Returns, and Risks

In general, micro, small, and medium enterprises are susceptible to the risks associated with innovation, manufacturing, and marketing due to diverse and unexplored problems, needs, and expected solutions (PNS factors) of consumers and market players in the competitive marketplace.

Resilience

The conventional entrepreneurial practices, embedded influence of family business, and myopic market orientation often encapsulate the entrepreneurial vision, operations, and performance. These factors contribute to develop resistance against change proneness among micro, small, and medium enterprises. Consequently, these enterprises are unable to develop competitive business models and become more pervasive to disrupt the legacy of family business practices and conventional technologies. The CTR factors also influence the entrepreneurial mindset and develop congruence with the new technology and business models by projecting the potential consumption, entrepreneurial benefits, and profitability (CBP factors). The combined effect of CTR factors and conventional entrepreneurial practices constitute the first order resilience in entrepreneurial operations against the disruptive drive of technology in changing market dynamics. The digital transformation of entrepreneurial activities constitutes the resilience towards second-order dynamic capabilities in contemporary entrepreneurial ecosystem (Roy et al., 2018). The availability of low capital and human resources, increasing manufacturing cost, and compatible pricing have significantly affected the entrepreneurial performance. These factors have critically contributed to developing entrepreneurial resilience in organizational and enterprise-driven market ecosystem. The entrepreneurial ecosystem in the contemporary context demands sensing of market potential for entrepreneurial products, exploring opportunities, co-creating consumer values, and transforming the entrepreneurial process to reduce the CTR factors and increase the CBP factors. The successful micro, small, and medium enterprises can align entrepreneurial operations by embracing low-cost innovation and technologies and reducing the resilience of both first and second orders (Khurana et al., 2022). The older legacy technologies, business models, operational processes, and entrepreneurial alliances with business partners often raise barriers in developing entrepreneurial compatibility with new business challenges like digital transformation of enterprises (Tortora et al., 2021).

The new generation micro, small, and medium enterprises adapting to technology-led business models face challenges in breaking emotional resilience due to lack of transformational leadership and managerial advocacy. These firms exhibit their will to transform entrepreneurial process but often remain under-resourced and evidence slow growth in the spur of digital technologies and innovation (Ardito et al., 2021). The internal resilience is commonly caused by the internal stakeholders comprising employees, managers, and leaders who lack in updated knowledge on changing technologies and market requirements. Consequently, micro, small, and medium enterprises are not adequately benefited to improve their dynamic capabilities towards the strategic change at both individual and organizational levels. However, the micro foundations of social enterprises tend to improve the entrepreneurial capabilities and competencies within the public policy programs in developing economies. An entrepreneurial firm that has overcome the first-order resilience gains internal strength to improve the dynamic capabilities by learning contemporary practices to adapt to disruptive entrepreneurial and business environments (Helfat & Raubitschek, 2018). Nonetheless, the entrepreneurial problem related to social and emotional intelligence often remains unexplained and unresolved to respond to the rapid and disruptive changes in market. These enterprises need to be protected from inherent uncertainties while their business operations should be geared up to adapt low-cost utilitarian technology-led innovations to respond to their resilient organizational behavior and drive higher-order dynamic capabilities to develop competitiveness. Overcoming the entrepreneurial resilience of conventional family business practices will encourage in building dynamic capabilities, which makes them more amenable to deal with changing consumer preferences and market competition (Doern et al., 2019).

Decision making in entrepreneurship is often associated with the unknown, partially known, or pre-calculated risk. The opaque outcomes of decision making attribute to CTR factors, which inculcate the personal resilience towards taking challenging decisions and experimenting new strategies. As entrepreneurs of most micro, small, and medium nurture their enterprises for self-employment, they refrain from experimental and less-promising approaches to operationalize despite the success of competing firms. Such resilience enhances barriers towards change proneness and perusing technology-led new ventures. However, the radical impact of resilience on new generation entrepreneurs in creating economic value, consistency in employment, and generating social and low-cost market innovations affect technology-led entrepreneurship (Alrawadieh et al., 2019). The attributes of R3 elements influencing entrepreneurial transformation have been illustrated in Fig. 3.2.

The evolution of micro, small, and medium enterprises embeds R3 elements comprising resilience, risk, and returns as experienced in the continuous growth alongside the technology and market dynamics. The resilience among entrepreneurs can be broadly classified into the first- and second-order functional resistance. The conventional wisdom and internal resilience develop fear of failure and occupational bias as first-order resilience among entrepreneurs. These factors lead to misalignment of CTR-CBP factors, which are further aggravated by the conditions of lack of knowledge, and inherent capabilities and competencies. The first-order resilience among entrepreneurs is provoked by the second-order elements of resilience comprising market disruption and mobilizing additional capital and human resources. Most enterprises face challenge in fund raising with the difficulty to explore angel investors to contribute venture capital and establish venture collaborations to transform the conventional enterprises. Besides these elements, economic viability and technological feasibility of enterprise expansion projects often push back the initiatives and increase the incubation time to transform entrepreneurial operations. Figure 3.2 demonstrates the entrepreneurial risk factors associated with the adoption of new technologies and drive digital transformation of existing operations of enterprises. In addition, the changing market dynamics and consumer preferences that demand for frugal innovation of products and services by using low-cost utilitarian technology often becomes complex proposition to micro, small, and medium enterprises. Most entrepreneurs have greater concern of long business break—even stages for new initiatives, which significantly affects the returns on investment and makes the business lifecycle shorter. Consequently, the fear of compromising with self-employment significantly increases with the entrepreneurs of these enterprises. Nonetheless, the entrepreneurial risk in transforming conventional enterprises with contemporary operations also grows with the INVUCA factors comprising investment risks, new products and services management, market vulnerability, behavioral uncertainties of consumers, decision complexities, and ambiguity in marketing strategies.

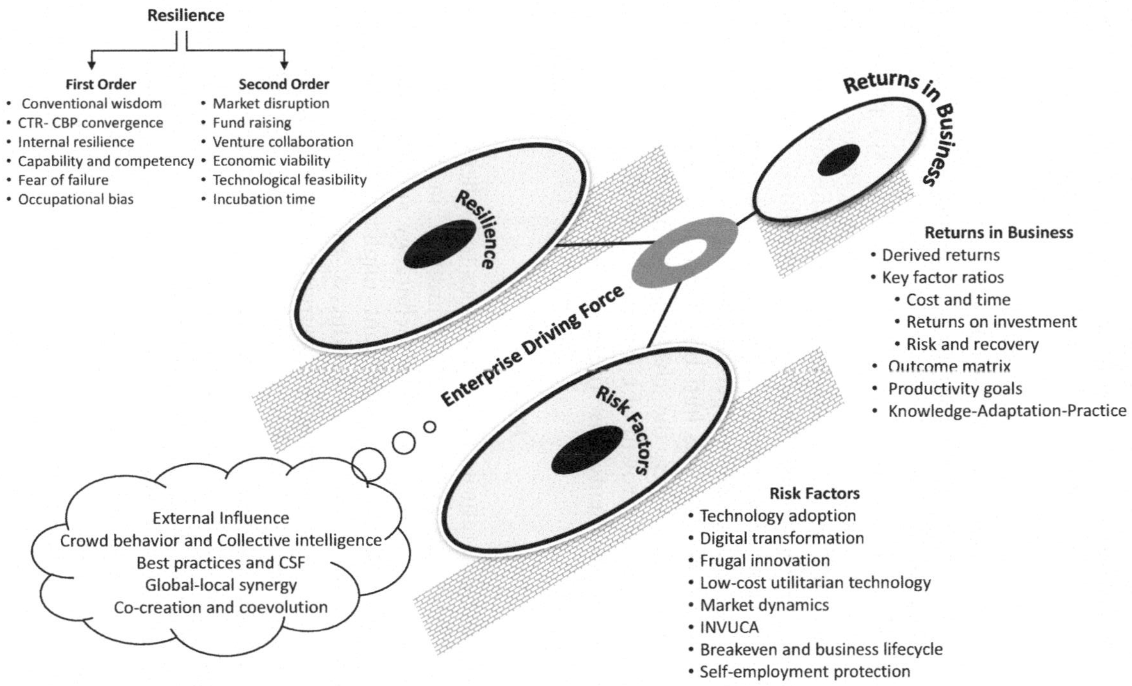

Fig. 3.2 Driving entrepreneurship with R3 elements (*Source* Authors)

Breaking the resilience and moving ahead with managing the entrepreneurial risk factors, entrepreneurs may experience the derived returns on investments in new initiatives with transformational practices. The returns in business can be measured in the context of key factor ratios of cost and time, investment and productivity, and risk and recovery to match with overall performance of enterprise. The returns in entrepreneurial business can be streamlined with the linear cohesiveness of knowledge (continuous learning), adaptation to changes, and improving managerial practices. These factors also affect the enterprise outcome matrix[1] for collaborative ventures among the key partners. In increasing returns in business, the enterprise driving force play critical role as illustrated in Fig. 3.2, which explains that the principal driving force consists of entrepreneurs deriving external influence to transform. The crowd behavior, collective intelligence, best practices, and critical success factors experienced by competing firms significantly motivate the conventional enterprises towards initiating the transformational process. Besides the above stimulants, the changing global–local synergy and patterns of contemporary growth of enterprises through co-creation and co-evolution also support enterprise transformation process.

Returns

Higher entrepreneurial returns are synonymous to higher entrepreneurial skills acquired through contemporary education in technology and market behavior. The perceived use of technology and embedded easiness in using technology have significant implications on increasing entrepreneurial returns in both products and services segment. Technology-based education stimulates entrepreneurs with higher levels of cognition and emotions to be the first to experiment and experience, value created innovation using low-cost technology. The factors seeking higher entrepreneurial returns include reducing CTR factors to gain higher risk premium in entrepreneurship, developing win–win strategic alliances in entrepreneurship, reducing occupational bias, creating value through differentiation, optimizing resource utilization, and implementing learned and acquired entrepreneurial skills through both formal education and informal education (Van Praag et al., 2013).

[1] Outcome Matrix of collaborative enterprises can be measured both qualitatively and quantitatively in reference to win-win, lose-lose, win-lose, and lose-win propositions.

Crowd behavior and collective intelligence push entrepreneurial cognition, emotions, and attitude in practicing market-oriented business model determined through evaluation of PNS factors and value creation perspectives. It can be argued that returns to technology-led entrepreneurship yield higher income for new generation entrepreneurs as compared to conventional family business-based entrepreneurs. Similarly, higher returns in micro, small, and medium enterprises are influenced by the creativity, collaboration, and convergence with market, which is driven by the internal and external stakeholders.

Most SME entrepreneurs develop design-to-market strategies in view of the lessons learned from market competition and their experience in managing niche market strategies, which help entrepreneurs in increasing their returns to entrepreneurial investment through systematic sales approaches. The design-to-market strategies over time become a common practice as the entrepreneurial marketing driven by low-cost innovation, high utilitarian value, and long-life cycle of entrepreneurial products in service. Accordingly, entrepreneurs follow bottom-up approach by choosing the target market or segment in the beginning and later explore the needs and demands of their targeted segment through personal relations to serve them efficiently by augmenting the returns to entrepreneurial products and services (Rajagopal, 2020a; Stokes, 2000). Ensuring entrepreneurial returns on investment involves cost-effective manufacturing, marketing, and value creation activities including market research. The frugal innovation products of micro enterprises are widely focused on digital marketing approaches, which are periodically supported by mass promotions strategies to increase entrepreneurial returns. However, entrepreneurs of small and medium business segment significantly depend on their personal networks to collect information about consumers and the market. These entrepreneurs heavily use consumer psychodynamics and the inter-personal communication such as word-of mouth to promote their products and services (Copley, 2013). The social facet of entrepreneurship education has closer proximity to innovation diffusion and business modeling than the formal teaching pedagogy or regulatory education to entrepreneurs. Though regulatory and social environment resources are external to entrepreneurship education, they can be purposely integrated and aligned with the entrepreneurial touchpoints to expand and enhance customers' journeys, customer experience, and marketability of their products or services in the emerging markets (Homburg et al., 2017; Rajagopal, 2020a).

Returns to entrepreneurship in micro, small, and medium enterprises are significantly influenced by the venture capital financing through angel investments and public policy programs. The resource utilization guided by the best practices and continuous learning contributes to higher entrepreneurial returns as compared to typical venture management skills acquired through family businesses in niche markets. The technology-driven enterprises receive collaborative venture financing and expand its entrepreneurial and business regime pushing the enterprises to new level towards public equity offering. Consequently, successful micro, small, and medium enterprises can raise public equity to reach higher-order corporate status. Skill-related continuous learning, reorientation of entrepreneurial knowledge, and acquiring best practices provide venture growth benefits to these enterprises' upscaling the business investment and turnover to provide higher returns to the enterprises. Harvesting own resources, learned and acquired skills, and ownership image in the marketplace provide consistent focus on entrepreneurial growth and enhancing possible returns in venture capital funded enterprises (Davidsson et al., 2009). Entrepreneurial returns, micro entrepreneurship, and self-employment are synonymous to socio-economic development in the region, which ensures employment and subsistence returns in developing economies. However, the returns to these enterprises are stimulated by providing additional resources at low cost through international institutions, government-driven FINTEC programs, non-government organizations (NGOs)-led programs, and private banks functioning at the grassroots. These institutions collaborate with entrepreneurs in developing micro-credit initiatives and business development programs irrespective of economic distress and productivity challenges (Gindling & Newhouse, 2014).

In the enterprise life cycle during the introductory stage, the entrepreneurial returns are lower or negative due to prolonged breakeven point. Most micro enterprises therefore have long incubation period within the niche market. The resource utilization matching to the productivity goals is one of the major challenges for micro, small, and medium enterprises to achieve targeted entrepreneurial returns. At this stage, managerial scholarship of entrepreneurs is critically low as they face major financial and market-related challenges besides the risks associated with the self-employment and liquidation of borrowed capital (Rajagopal & Behl, 2023). Incubation of innovations has emerged as a new model of start-up facilitation in most developing economies. Venture capitalists review the incubators and assess the projected growth and profitability in businesses to invest. The venture capitalists review the incubators to diversify risky investment portfolios, while the prospecting entrepreneurs approach the incubators to review the economically viable and technologically feasible support for start-up projects. Entrepreneurial incubators face both challenges and opportunities to grow competitive enterprises considering the embedded investment and entrepreneurial risks. Broadly, there are five incubator archetypes such as the university incubator, the independent commercial incubator, the regional business incubator, the company-internal incubator, and the virtual incubator (Carayannis & von Zedtwitz, 2005). Innovations of local origin are attracted to the global companies as they plan to bring back the local innovation, which is largely frugal in nature, to the mass-market. Therefore, the relational embeddedness of large companies with the external MSMEs appears to be essential for the evolution of local innovations to the global scale. Turning local innovations into global brands can be identified as innovativeness evoked by the large companies or their subsidiaries at the bottom-of-the-pyramid. However, in this process, transfer of reverse knowledge in the functional areas is a critical perspective (Isaac et al., 2019; Rajagopal & Behl, 2023).

Risk

Transforming conventional entrepreneurial business practices to innovative and market-oriented business model demands creating superior customer and enterprise value by involving stakeholders and market players such as supply chain and packaging partners. Market-oriented business model of micro, small, and medium enterprises broadly address societal, commercial, and environmental needs through integrated business operations. Ecosystems of different business models are specific to entrepreneurial goals, which determine its corporate image and operational posture within the industry. Some enterprises that grow with social innovation objectives have a greater number of value-based designs encompassing social needs, stakeholder education, user value generation, and bridging the corporate social responsibilities. Transformational entrepreneurship manifests itself in corporate culture, organizational behavior, and functional practices of companies. Consequently, such entrepreneurial business model is spread longitudinally; so, they are bound to face unforeseen risks which need to be managed in association with the stakeholders. However, companies must engage in mapping the performance of pilot business-experimentation models (Rajagopal, 2021). However, in implementing market-oriented business models, the transforming enterprises face complexity for alignment of value, diverging interests, investment risks, profitability, and corporate responsibilities. Multi-stakeholder engagement in implementing collaborative entrepreneurship enhances the risks in operations and perceived profit goals. Entrepreneurs perceive high risk of engaging in the activities targeted towards new business models, entrepreneurial postures, and establishing brand value in short term as it takes a long time to achieve predetermined profit goals, create consumer value, and develop convergence with social responsibilities. The transaction cost theory explains the links between company's reputation, degree of risk, and effective cost of production (Tate et al., 2011).

The micro, small, and medium enterprises anticipate short-run returns on investment made in transformational entrepreneurial projects. Therefore, integrating technology-led entrepreneurial projects into market-oriented business model(s) is the contemporary option for these enterprises. Among the elements of business canvas, measuring cost-time-risk (CTR factors), key partners, possible shared resources, predetermined revenue stream and its management, social value generation, investment on social innovation, and analyzing market trends make significant contributions (Rajagopal, 2021). The collaborative entrepreneurship is an emerging trend to develop alliance with large companies and promote global–local business synergy for entrepreneurial growth. However, often collaborative enterprises face mismatch of corporate goals and workplace practices, which disrupt the purpose of alliance and become defunct. The complexity in developing such alliances require aligning objectives to perceive the stakeholder and business values by converging divergent operational interests of collaborating firms, lowering risks, and increasing accountability to connect efficiently with the existing processes and activities. Openness for strategic alignment of business models with stakeholder needs, culture, and societal values significantly affect the implementation of sustainable business models (Velter et al., 2020).

The transforming enterprises, irrespective of the scale of business in local market, face challenges and risks in building appropriate innovation ecosystems to carry out the innovation business projects successfully. Leveraging tasks within the predetermined innovation ecosystem reduces various risks related to the manufacturing, project process, and commercialization. Random innovations are characterized by the fundamental types of risk that encompass innovation initiative risks, which are the familiar uncertainties of managing a project; interdependence risks comprising uncertainties of coordinating with alliance or outsourced innovators or start-up enterprises; and integration risks causing the uncertainties occurring during the adoption process across the innovation value chain. Firms that work within the innovation ecosystem, could assess risks holistically in an innovative business project, and systematically establish realistic expectations develop a more refined set of environmental contingencies, and arrive at a more robust innovation strategy could make the innovation successful (Adner, 2006; Rajagopal, 2016). Choice of technology in business models are subjected to the analysis of economic viability (cost, time, risk, and use value) and feasibility (applied attributes, technology lifecycle, and functional complementarity). Furthermore, the availability of solid and liquid waste for recycling (including dump management), manufacturing and maintenance processes, opportunities of co-evolution of sustainability projects, and co-creating values also contribute to the domains of technology and market, business modeling, and social drivers.

One of the principal macroeconomic factors is resources and investment planning, which not only ensures funding possibilities of sustainability projects, but also aims at reducing the costs of acquiring information, enforcing contracts, manufacturing, and making transactions. Micro, small, and medium enterprises are also susceptible to INVUCA risks in the business. INVUCA constitutes investment risks, new products and services management, market vulnerability, behavioral uncertainties of consumers, decision complexities, and ambiguity in marketing strategies. Although the digital marketing strategies can enable such ventures, the managerial approach taken towards business is the real differentiator (Rajagopal, 2019). Local entrepreneurs in collaboration with key partners, engaged in manufacturing and marketing of frugal innovation products, tend to uncover opportunities and risks in new markets, set priorities, and generate consumer awareness through digital networks and marketing programs. Consequently, these enterprises can be developed by analyzing the market behavior to identify opportunities for promoting business growth through the following strategies:

- Developing low-cost innovative products
- Identifying new consumer segments (preferably *big middle*)

- Developing new business portfolios
- Improving return on capital through market taxonomy (B-to-B, B-to-C, C-to-C, and O-to-O)
- Improving and managing value chains in supply and retail operations
- Managing capital risk and operational contingencies.

Systematic assessments of the risks and opportunities in market-oriented business model help local enterprises and international companies to develop competitive strategies to manage the cost-revenue contingencies.

Change Management

Transformational entrepreneurship, which adapts to contemporary changes in technology, market, and management, aims at contributing to improved entrepreneurial practices. New practices by micro, small, and medium enterprises, tuned to dynamic business conditions of globalization, digitization, and environmentalism have evolved in view of the developments discussed above. Change management practices in enterprises adhere largely to technology-led manufacturing and marketing models. A change is needed today in local enterprises to understand, practice, and adapt to next generation entrepreneurial practices integrating frugal innovations, utilitarian values, adaptable technologies by users, and in developing ability to collaborate with large enterprises to upscale entrepreneurial business. The entrepreneurial scholarship can benefit in future from the dynamics of new generation technology driven by AI, ML, and LLM towards creating entrepreneurial growth and customer value.

The new generation enterprises at local and regional level serving the competitive markets face threats from the new entrants, with technology-driven innovation to disrupt the business of low-cost competitors. Successful enterprises employ several short-term tactics like focusing minimum viable consumer segments, delivering the basic benefits better than rivals, and maintaining low prices with super-efficient operations. The price-quality relationship and perceived value of consumers tend to disrupt the normal buying behavior towards frugal innovation products of micro, small, and medium enterprises in both local and regional markets. Large companies with wider market share and adequate resources take various approaches to compete against cut-price players. Some differentiate their products, while others launch low-cost products encouraging price war as solutions to overcome the market competition (Kumar, 2006). The rapidly increasing manufacturing and marketing technology enhances the operational complexities and the rate of change in market behavior significantly affects the performance of these enterprises in competitive markets. As micro enterprises have dramatically increased over the years, these enterprises find it increasingly difficult to cope up with the speed of change and manage the enterprise performance compatible to the demand for products and services, and match enterprise-market requirements to stay competitive. With continuously increasing market competition, there exists the problem of improving forecasting to increase product development agility. These strategies can help firms to restructure their manufacturing, marketing, and operations processes by adapting to agile management practices, and sustain in the turbulent market conditions (Rajagopal, 2020b). The action stages of change management path for micro, small, and medium enterprises are depicted in Fig. 3.3.

Change management is a difficult subject to be perused by micro, small, and medium enterprises due to various psychological and economic perspectives, which trigger substantial risk and uncertainty. However, the outcomes of change management ensure higher profit, provide alternate revenue schema, and are able to create value by engaging internal and external stakeholders as illustrated in Fig. 3.3. In this process, the fundamental challenge is to motivate entrepreneurs to design and implement change management in the enterprise. Many entrepreneurial support organizations in developing economies have pooled motivational resources and created knowledge hubs, which demonstrate contemporary research and development for continuous learning and acquiring new skills. The changing dynamics within industry and entrepreneurial incubators instituted by various academic institutions in collaboration with industries also serve as entrepreneurial stimulators, which motivate the change management among entrepreneurs. The role of academic institutions, industries, incubators, and the knowledge hubs helps in widening entrepreneurial vision to enhance their proximity to market, creating innovative products and services to stay competitive in market, and develop transformational leadership to reestablish a progressive entrepreneurial image. These factors significantly affect the entrepreneurial mindset, which re-orient them towards change management and refine attitude by analyzing both the internal and external influences. The transformational leadership plays a critical role in reforming entrepreneurial mindset through effective leader-member

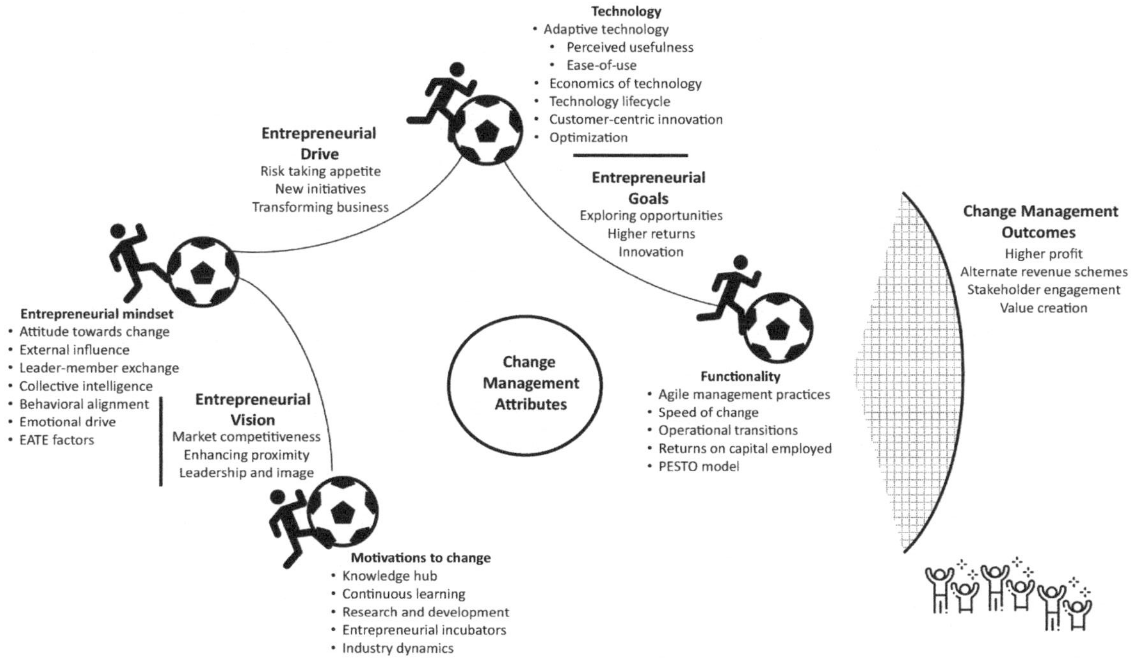

Fig. 3.3 Change management journey of micro, small, and medium enterprises (*Source* Authors)

exchange, which helps in streamlining entrepreneurial behavior towards change management and guides cognitive alignment with contemporary market ecosystem. EATE factors consisting of *expertise*, *accountability*, *trust* in partnership, and *experience* derived from the change management concept motivate entrepreneurs to initiate organizational restructuring by creating a new sense of belongingness among leaders, employees, consumers, and stakeholders. The convergence of organizational and personal attributes creates emotional drive to reaffirm the need for change management process among entrepreneurs. The PESTO model comprising *performance* effectiveness, entrepreneurial *earning*, *sharing* profit with partners, managing productivity-based *transformation*, and developing cost-effective *operational* efficiency significantly supports the change management process to achieve entrepreneurial goals. Successfully implementing the change management process helps micro, small, and medium enterprises to explore new opportunities and diversify production in business operations to gain higher returns by managing innovations for different consumer segments.

Adapting to new technology in managing changes in entrepreneurial process requires significant risk-taking appetite among entrepreneurs. Such entrepreneurial drive will push new initiatives and designing strategies for transforming the entrepreneurial production in business processes. The technology acceptance model can fit well into the change management process as entrepreneurs orient towards adapting to new technologies and digitization based on the perceived usefulness to technology change and associated ease of use. Besides these technology acceptance perspectives, the change management in enterprises is significantly affected by the economics of technology (CTR and CBP factors) and technology lifecycle (longevity, perceived use value, and commercial value for money). The major challenge for micro, small, and medium enterprises to initiate change management process is to optimize production and business processes in the context of investment, cost effectiveness, and expected outcome. However, optimizing these factors appears to be complex in dynamic market environment and practice customer-centric innovation with low cost and risk. On streamlining entrepreneurial motivations to change management, enhancing entrepreneurial vision, revamping entrepreneurial mindset, and developing entrepreneurial drive to adopt technology and new entrepreneurial goals lead to demonstrate improved functionality of the enterprises. Successfully initiating the change management process using agile practices will improve the operational transitions and ensure returns on capital employed. Nevertheless, entrepreneurs need to monitor the speed of change during transition process to ensure desired benefits of change management.

Increasing breakthrough innovations and rapidly changing information and communication technologies have a ruthless effect on conventional micro, small, and medium enterprises, which has forced them to radically change their manufacturing, marketing, and management practices to survive within the industry. The business culture today upholds operational values of firms that have transformed with the changing technology and could establish new value propositions for internal and external stakeholders. These enterprises require organizational restructuring by exploring dynamic talent and cohesive workplace environment with team structures in lieu of person-oriented task management. Such change management calls for improved leader-member exchange with shared accountability, collective decisions, and multilayered task management organizational culture. Consequently, these enterprises need to develop operational innovations to emulate and explore convergent strategies with competitors within the industry and business ecosystem. The change management among these enterprises must be disruptive in nature, and focused on competitive growth and strategic enterprise goals to ensure superior performance in the marketplace (Hammer, 2004). Commonly, micro, small, and medium enterprises defer to implement change management practices due to the embedded risk of high-cost experimentation, which might damper their reputation within niche market and damage their brand image. However, collaboration with relatively large companies on technology might reduce the complexity in experimenting technologies to assure low-cost innovation of utilitarian products to serve predetermined consumer segments. One of the major challenges in adapting to technology-led change management is that it affects the 360-degree operational processes by elevating the risk regimes. Nonetheless, enterprise transformations irrespective of the scale of operations often raise a pertinent question on their rate of success. It has been observed that technology-led transformations incur high cost in developing operational skills among human resources. Such transformations have a miserable success rate at the grassroots among micro and small enterprises, as they either fail to deliver the anticipated benefits or are led to bankruptcy due to flawed implementation of change management practices (Anand & Barsoux, 2017).

The change management practices in production and business operations in micro, small, and medium enterprises face major challenges in revamping their business models to achieve desired level of entrepreneurial performance. The trends in business modeling have been shifting rapidly since the mid-twentieth century from supply-led (manufacture oriented) to demand-driven (customer centric) to crowd-based business modeling. Such change has been a global phenomenon, which has seeded the concept of agile modeling in doing business in competitive marketplace. Companies face various organizational and operational challenges while transitioning to the agile functional model. Among many complexities, identifying and driving business units to adapt to the agile management culture by engineering multifunctional teams and developing new management practices that are compatible cause major concern to the companies to sustain the agile management practices (Chen et al., 2016). Despite the above fundamental concerns, the agile functional model has been adopted by many companies and received increased attention in academic research. There are various dimensions of business agility that affect the performance of firms. The agility in business includes workplace culture, decision making, operations, technology, innovation, and customer behavior at the bottom line comprising people, profit, and sustainability. Understanding people is connected to the personality, social values, and ethnicity. Advances in digital technologies have increased the possibilities of developing agile business models by outsourcing business activities to crowds comprising contributors (Rajagopal, 2022).

Entrepreneurial agility is one of the emerging change management agents, which is value-driven, project-oriented, and flexible process to develop entrepreneurial strategies. The attributes of dynamic capability of a company of re-aligning and re-deploying its resources to create value to manage continuity in business uncertainty and changes in business operations form the foundation of entrepreneurial agility. Change management interventions are systematically synchronized to facilitate planned change in manufacturing, marketing, and operational processes. Broadly the change management interventions can be classified as indicated below:

- Systematic change in communication process leading to information dissemination, structuring of communication, and deriving contents out of dialogic communication.

- Managing active involvement of internal and external stakeholders towards consultation, co-creation, and collective decision making to plan and implement predetermined change management practices.
- Developing knowledge management infrastructure to support training and skill development for employees.
- Planning rewards and goal setting for implementing change management in phases.
- Exploring role models and peer exchange platforms to reinforce change management practices.

The change management interventions if implemented systematically influence employee's cognition, emotions, and motivations to implement and monitor the planned changes in the enterprise. Such employee orientation tends to enhance the peer capabilities and competencies to explore new opportunities for co-created innovations and customer-centric growth of enterprises (Hagl et al., 2024).

Previous research studies on influence maximization through the network structure reveal that though the advancement of information technology has significantly stimulated the process of extensive social relationship, it has grown complex with the multi-dimensional characteristics of communication. The degree of influence maximization has a direct relationship with the quality of social network data, its usage, and behavioral alignment with the collective intelligence generation through the social media channels. The crowd influence seeks to change the individual consumption behavior under a social network propagation pattern. Effective online social networks such as Twitter and Facebook have rapidly grown and integrated with the lives of people (Hautz et al., 2017). Change management interventions can be initiated within or outside the organization engaging internal and external stakeholders. The collective intelligence derived through social networks also plays as change agents to be adapted to the existing enterprise environment. Change management interventions are systematized activities executed by an organizational actor, who can be the change manager to facilitate planned change by analyzing the collective intelligence and crowd influence. The workplace interventions can substantially improve the organizational efficiency and well-being of employees and stakeholders affecting the overall performance (Stouten et al., 2018). Consequently, many social network users share information with other members in a routine agenda, generating mass data being used by the organizations to create value for marketing, rumor detection, public opinion analysis, and managing many social causes. Such rapidly evolving blend of information and emotion embeds the crowd mood of individuals and the diffusion of communication process. The social communication and learning on thematic interests are aggressive behavioral processes, which are carried out until the crowd or community mood reaches an equilibrium. The mode of information propagation caused by the user structure and emotion has a wider outreach and emotional drive. Studies have found that the emotional information is easier to propagate through the social networks even by using the non-verbal emoji symbols (Rajagopal, 2022).

Agile entrepreneurial practices help firms in creating and protecting customer value for attaining high market share and profit through integrating the activities within the business ecosystem. The success of agile entrepreneurship has been observed in developing and launching of advertising campaigns. These activities can be operationalized, reviewed, and aligned with the market requirements to ensure high performance. In the change management process, teams periodically evaluate the efficiency of the process and eliminate redundancy to align and optimize production and business operations accordingly. Emerging enterprises engaged in agile practices tend to achieve higher customer engagement and value and an increased ability to adapt to market uncertainties, and change stimulate speed towards developing business competitiveness. Previous studies argue that the response of the firms to co-creation and customer-driven opportunities depends on the intensity of competition and the degree of cannibalizing the market share by the competitive firms. Consequently, implementing change management practices, enterprises need to focus on responding quickly to the customer-centric innovation and competitive strategies (Rajagopal, 2022).

In implementing the change management practices, enterprises at local and regional level need to check organizational structure, which could support the implementation of changes in production, business, and processes. Most micro, small, and medium enterprises possess inadequate organizational structure to capitalize on the benefits of change management and explore new opportunities in emerging markets. Locating customer facing processes in developing economies parallel to systematic corporate structures is a major challenge to exploit both temporal and spatial benefits on implementing change management practices. This requires optimizing organizational structures by segmenting knowledge hubs and research and development incubators both vertically and horizontally within the enterprises (*e.g.*, Kumar & Puranam, 2011). The competitive performance of the firm is significantly driven by the changing customer needs. The change management practices influence firm's performance to manage market complexity with flexible strategies. Effective implementation of strategies with such practices needs firms to develop abilities on sensing the dynamics of industry, market, operational flexibility, speed of change, and market responsiveness. These attributes allow enterprises to co-create and co-evolve with customer-centric strategies in a changing environment and respond rapidly to the complexities by reconfiguring their change management practices. Entrepreneurs work with the improved enterprise management practices, which respond to contemporary challenges and changing trends in business (Xu et al., 2018). Change management processes tend to easily adjust plans and strategies for responding swiftly to new opportunities and the emerging challenges. While managing technology-led enterprises and co-creating low-cost innovations, they work with social media channels in the interactive digital market environment, which demands entrepreneurial agility. Implementing flexible strategies, micro, small, and medium enterprises develop convergence with the crowd behavior and social consciousness of customers. Agile methodology (Gera et al., 2019) is also considered for designing and implementing change management practices as an alternative to Waterfall methodology—the rigid, top-down approach to project management that most marketers follow.

References

Adner, R. (2006). Match Your Innovation Strategy to Your Innovation Ecosystem. *Harvard Business Review, 83*(4), 98–116.

Alrawadieh, Z., Karayilan, E., & Cetin, G. (2019). Understanding the challenges of refugee entrepreneurship in tourism and hospitality. *Service Industries Journal, 39*(9–10), 717–740.

Anand, N. and Barsoux, J.-L. (2017, November–December). what everyone gets wrong about change management. *Harvard Business Review*, 78–85.

Ardito, L., Raby, S., Albino, V., & Bertoldi, B. (2021). The duality of digital and environmental orientations in the context of SMEs: Implications for innovation performance. *Journal of Business Research, 123*, 44–56.

Bae, T.J., Qian, S., Miao, C., & Fiet, J.O. (2014). The relationship between entrepreneurship education and entrepreneurial intentions: A meta-analytical review. *Entrepreneurship: Theory and Practice, 38*(2), 217–254.

Buratti, N., Sillig, C., & Albanese, M. (2022). Community enterprise, community entrepreneurship and local development: A literature review on three decades of empirical studies and theorizations. *Entrepreneurship & Regional Development, 34*(5–6), 376–401.

Copley, P. (2013). The need to deliver higher-order skills in the context of marketing in SMEs. *Industry and Higher Education, 27*(6), 465–476.

Carayannis, E. G., & von Zedtwitz, M. (2005). Architecting gloCal (global–local), real-virtual incubator networks (G-RVINs) as catalysts and accelerators of entrepreneurship in transitioning and developing economies: Lessons learned and best practices from current development and business incubation practices. *Technovation, 25*(2), 95–110.

Chen, R., Ravichandar, R., & Proctor, D. (2016). Managing the transition to the new agile business and product development model: Lessons from Cisco Systems. *Business Horizons, 59*(6), 635–644.

Davidsson, P., Steffens, P., & Fitzsimmons, J. (2009). Growing profitable or growing from profits: Putting the horse in front of the cart? *Journal of Business Venture, 24*(4), 388–406.

Doern, R., Williams, N., & Vorley, T. (2019). Special issue on entrepreneurship and crises: Business as usual? An introduction and review of the literature. *Entrepreneurship & Regional Development, 31*(5–6), 400–412.

Gera, G., Gera, B., & Mishra, A. (2019). Role of Agile marketing in the present era. *International Journal of Technical Research & Science, 4*(5), 40–44.

Gindling, T. H., & Newhouse, D. (2014). Self-employment in the developing world. *World Development, 56*(1), 313–331.

Graham, B., & Bonner, K. (2024). The role of institutions in early-stage entrepreneurship: An explainable artificial intelligence approach. *Journal of Business Research*, 175. https://doi.org/10.1016/j.jbusres.2024.114567

Hagl, C., Kanitz, R., Gonzalez, K., & Hoegl, M. (2024). Change management interventions: Taking stock and moving forward. *Human Resource Management Review, 34*(1), https://doi.org/10.1016/j.hrmr.2023.101000

Hautz, J., Seidl, D., & Whittington, R. (2017). Open strategy: Dimensions, dilemmas, dynamics. *Long Range Planning, 50*(3), 298–309.

Hammer, M. (2004). Deep change: How Operational innovation can transform your company. *Harvard Business Review, 82*(4), 84–93.

Helfat, E. C., & Raubitschek, R. S. (2018). Dynamic and integrative capabilities for profiting from innovation in digital platform-based ecosystems. *Research Policy, 47*(8), 1391–1399.

Homburg, C., Jozić, D., & Kuehnl, C. (2017). Customer experience management: Toward implementing an evolving marketing concept. *Journal of the Academy of Marketing Science, 45*(3), 377–401.

Isaac, V. R., Borini, F. M., Raziq, M. M., & Benito, G. R. G. (2019). From local to global innovation: The role of subsidiaries' external relational embeddedness in an emerging market. *International Business Review, 28*(4), 638–646.

Jiang, Y., & Zheng, W. (2021). Coupling mechanism of green building industry innovation ecosystem based on blockchain smart city. *Journal of Cleaner Production*, 307. https://doi.org/10.1016/j.jclepro.2021.126766

Kayes, A. B., Kayes, D. C., & Kolb, D. A. (2005). Experiential learning in teams. *Simulation and Gaming, 36*(3), 330–354.

Khurana, I., Dutta, D. K., & Ghura, A. S. (2022). SMEs and digital transformation during a crisis: The emergence of resilience as a second-order dynamic capability in an entrepreneurial ecosystem. *Journal of Business Research, 150*, 623–641.

Kumar, N. (2006). Strategies to fight low-cost rivals. *Harvard Business Review, 84*, (12), 104–112.

Kumar, N., & Puranam, P. (2011). Have you restructured for global success? *Harvard Business Review, 83*(10), 123–128.

La Guardia, D., Gentile, M., Grande, V. D., Ottaviano, S., & Allegra, M. (2014). A game based learning model for entrepreneurship education. *Procedia—Social and Behavioral Sciences, 141*, 195–199.

Liu, S. C.-H. & Lee, T. (2019). The multilevel effects of transformational leadership on entrepreneurial orientation and service innovation. *International Journal of Hospitality Management, 82*, 278–286

Rajagopal. (2016). *Innovative business projects: Breaking complexities, building performance (Vol. 1)—Fundamentals and project environment*. Business Expert Press.

Rajagopal. (2019). *Contemporary marketing strategy: Analyzing consumer behavior to drive managerial decision making*. Palgrave Macmillan.

Rajagopal. (2020a). *Entrepreneurship, education, and economics: A Helix effect on business growth*. In Rajagopal & Behl, R. (Eds.). Entrepreneurship and regional development: Analyzing growth models in emerging markets (pp. 3–24). Palgrave Macmillan.

Rajagopal. (2020b). *Transgenerational marketing: Evolution, expansion, and experience*. Palgrave Macmillan.

Rajagopal. (2021). *Sustainable businesses in developing economies—Socio-economic and governance perspectives*. Palgrave Macmillan.

Rajagopal. (2022). *Agile marketing strategies—New approaches to engaging consumer behavior*. Springer.

Rajagopal & Behl, R. (2023). *Paradigm shift in business—Critical appraisal of agile management practices*. Springer, Palgrave Macmillan.

Roy, R., Lampert, C. M., & Stoyneva, I. (2018). When dinosaurs fly: The role of firm capabilities in the 'avianization' of incumbents during disruptive technological change. *Strategic Entrepreneurship Journal, 12*(2), 261–284.

Schleicher, J., Vögler, M., Dustdar, S., & Inzinger, C. (2016). Enabling a Smart City Application Ecosystem: Requirements and Architectural Aspects. *IEEE Internet Computing, 20*(2), 58–65.

Stokes, D. (2000). Putting entrepreneurship into marketing: The process of entrepreneurial marketing. *Journal of Research in Marketing and Entrepreneurship, 2*(1), 1–16.

Stouten, J., Rousseau, D. M., & De Cremer, D. (2018). Successful organizational change: Integrating the management practice and scholarly literatures. *Academy of Management Annals, 12*(2), 752–788.

Tate, W. L., Dooley, K. J., & Ellram, L. M. (2011). Transaction cost and institutional drivers of supplier adoption of environmental practices. *Journal of Business Logistics, 32*(1), 6–16.

Tortora, D., Chierici, R., Briamonte, M. F., & Tiscini, R. (2021). 'I digitize so I exist'. Searching for critical capabilities affecting firms' digital innovation. *Journal of Business Research, 129*, 193–204.

Van Praag, M., van Witteloostuijn, A., & van der Sluis, J. (2013). The higher returns to formal education for entrepreneurs versus employees. *Small Business Economics, 40*(2), 375–396.

Velter, M. G. E., Bitzer, V., Bocken, N. M. P., & Kemp, R. (2020). Sustainable business model innovation: The role of boundary work for multi-stakeholder alignment. *Journal of Cleaner Production*, 247. https://doi.org/10.1016/j.jclepro.2019.119497

Xu, H., Guo, H., Zhang, J., & Dang, A. (2018). Facilitating dynamic marketing capabilities development for domestic and foreign firms in an emerging economy. *Journal of Business Research, 86*, 141–152.

CHAPTER 4

The Game Changer Models

Abstract This chapter exhibits 'the game map' plotting five game changer models comprising local area technology and innovation for transformation and ubiquitous development of entrepreneurship (LATITUDE), growth and acceleration in restructuring accountable gender entrepreneurship (GARAGE), and revamping innovation for social entrepreneurship (RISE). Other two game changer models identified as social ubiquity of innovation and technology in entrepreneurship (SUIT-E) and global accessibility to markets and entrepreneurship in a digital interphase (GAME-DI) are also discussed as critical game changers contributing to the transformation of conventional entrepreneurship to technology-driven and market-oriented entrepreneurial business model. These game changer models have been evaluated from the perspective of value propositions, collective intelligence, extent of business transformation, environmental mining, and latent opportunities and threat. The above game changer models are significant in entrepreneurial development as a critical component of social and economic evolution in the current innovation and technology ecosystems. The importance of the proposed models has potential to spark interest of government in developing economies to design compatible public programs to improve capability and competency of local enterprises (e.g., Pérez-Pérez, C et al., 2021).

Rajagopal and A. Rajagopal, *Unmasking Invisible Challenges in Entrepreneurship*, Palgrave Studies of Entrepreneurship and Social Challenges in Developing Economies,
https://doi.org/10.1007/978-3-031-63653-0_4

Keywords Growth · Acceleration · Technology · Innovation · Transformation · Ubiquitous development · Social entrepreneurship · Gender · Global accessibility · Marketing · Digital interface

This chapter exhibits 'the game map' plotting five game changer models comprising local area technology and innovation, for transformation and ubiquitous development of entrepreneurship (LATITUDE), growth and acceleration in restructuring accountable gender entrepreneurship (GARAGE), and revamping innovation for social entrepreneurship (RISE). Other two game changer models identified as social ubiquity of innovation and technology in entrepreneurship (SUIT-E) and global accessibility to markets and entrepreneurship in a digital interface (GAME-DI) are also discussed as critical game changers contributing to the transformation of conventional entrepreneurship to technology-driven and market-oriented entrepreneurial business model. These game changer models have been evaluated from the perspective of value propositions, collective intelligence, extent of business transformation, environmental mining, and latent opportunities and threat.

The Game Map

Continuous innovation and technology are the principal change agents in transforming entrepreneurship to converge with the local and global entrepreneurial attributes. The creativity in entrepreneurship has two dimensions, which include the innate attributes and crowd stimulation for new venture ideation (Kier & McMullen, 2020). The local area technology and innovation in entrepreneurial products and services have co-created ideas, which support new generation markets and offer projected evaluations on consumer preferences and market demand. The collective ideation process has wider proximity to cater to consumer needs and markets by involving multiple stakeholders consisting of undetermined crowd, employees, consumers, financial institutions, and angel investors. These internal and external stakeholders constitute a team to guide entrepreneurs in the process of developing competitive entrepreneurship and catering to the market with differentiation (Kier & McMullen, 2018). These change agents help in conducting participatory entrepreneurial appraisal for ubiquitous development of entrepreneurship by transforming the conventional innovation and technology to cater to local areas and bridge the local enterprises with wider area network. These game changing elements tend to transform the organizational culture of micro, small, and medium enterprises and develop a synchronized composition of activities related to innovation, technology, and market competitiveness to develop an effective business model as compared to conventional wisdom. The collective cognitive skills and the intervention of entrepreneurial change agents stimulate local enterprises to evaluate their capabilities and competencies and map their requirements for necessary skill development. The optimal mix of entrepreneurial business requires an efficient use of resources to make strategic decisions and prepare micro enterprises with both the technical and non-technical backgrounds to compete with the contemporary market strengths and threats. By periodically conducting entrepreneurial appraisal, these enterprises can map their weaknesses to overcome, develop strengths, and explore new opportunities to stay differentiated. The entrepreneurial differentiators such as attributes of products and services, utilitarian and hedonic values, price-quality relationship, effects of brand and ethnicity, and associated social values provide multiple pathways in practicing entrepreneurship with high-performing configuration in contemporary marketplace (Frederiks et al., 2019).

The intervention of key partners and critical change agents comprising entrepreneurial education, technology transfer, ideation and innovation, institutional finance, and public policy programs broadly defines the business constructs of micro, small, and medium enterprises. These change agents develop reliable and valid measures to position the local enterprises with quality differentiation and competitive venture attributes in the marketplace. These enterprises tend to portray their innovation as unique ethnic skills to derive highest empathy of consumers to stay competitive in the marketplace (McMullen, 2015). The new ideas acquired through collective intelligence help micro, small, and medium enterprises to transform their design thinking unequivocally, conduct pilot testing of innovative products, and remove cognitive biases in consumption of low-cost entrepreneurial products. These factors significantly contribute to growth and acceleration in restructuring accountable entrepreneurship (Mmbaga et al., 2020). There is an increasing concern on the role of gender in entrepreneurship and the associated success and failure rates. The governments in developing economies have generated enormous social consciousness towards inclusivity and diversity in entrepreneurship and supported this philosophy with effective public policy programs which also gained international appreciation. The entrepreneurship has broad and diverse scope with focus on gender-based initiatives that create differences across male and female entrepreneurs' performance through technological interventions and profit regimes. Therefore, growth and acceleration of entrepreneurship have direct impact on gender-led entrepreneurship. The women entrepreneurs face specific challenges like work-life balance, self-confidence in managing entrepreneurial carrier, and ensuring high growth rate. Commonly, most women-led start-ups face initial lower growth potential owing to family obligations and economic contingencies (Guzman & Kacperczyk, 2019).

Information and communication technologies provided extensive networking of social entrepreneurs to achieve social and financial goals. Combining conventional business models with a clear social perspective helps social enterprises to promote both for-profit and not-for-profit organizations to achieve social and financial objectives. Utilizing the available public technologies, social enterprises have accessed larger and diversified entrepreneurial operations to reach out the underprivileged socio-economic demographics. These enterprises are engaged in developing social products and services to transform social systems and cater to the well-being of the communities through reinvestment of their revenues (Kamran et al., 2022). Most social enterprises follow innovation-based growth model with collective social capital that influences social innovation and consequently economic growth. Social capital stimulates innovation activities, which leads to higher profits if appropriately commercialized. Such market-led innovation results into higher social capital and reinforcing social benefits and values. Social enterprises are evolved with stakeholders to serve the urban and rural demographics, which also serve the underprivileged consumers in a weak regulatory framework. In emerging markets, customers and members of social enterprises at the bottom-of-the-pyramid are targeted for the basic benefits and services such as healthcare, education, and farm and non-farm activities. Social entrepreneurs use innovative business models to build solutions with the available resources and offer basic services to the stakeholders in a sustainable way. The principal objective of social enterprises is to create social impact and generate economic and social values in a sustainable manner (Mair and Schoen, 2007; Rajagopal, 2021a). Therefore, it can be stated that social enterprises significantly contribute to welfare economics pertaining to the communities at the bottom of the pyramid and develop the sense of social well-being and ubiquitous economic development. However, social entrepreneurship is constantly facing challenges to be resolved and to overcome the high levels of uncertainty in transforming opportunities to a social and business stimulator. Social entrepreneurship today requires revamping holistically in the context of innovation, technology, and sustainability (Sarasvathy, 2021).

There are broadly five game changer synergies, which have complex attributes and need to be synchronized to map the holistic effects of these game changer domains. The five domains, which play catalytic role in changing the conventional enterprise market game, are exhibited in Fig. 4.1 that are categorically listed below:

- LATITUDE—Local Area Technology and Innovation for Transformation and Ubiquitous Development of Entrepreneurship.
- GARAGE—Growth and Acceleration in Restructuring Accountable Gender Entrepreneurship.
- RISE—Revamping Innovation for Social Entrepreneurship.
- SUIT-E—Social Ubiquity of Innovation and Technology in Entrepreneurship.
- GAME-DI—Global Accessibility to Markets and Entrepreneurship in a Digital Interface.

The meticulous planning of local area technology to support frugal innovation and transform entrepreneurship for ubiquitous development can be achieved in working through the LATITUDE domain. This domain embodies multi-tasking skills to transform conventional entrepreneurial practices through continuous innovation converging with changing market demand and consumer preferences. The crowd interface through digital networks supports entrepreneurial ideation and design thinking process through collective intelligence, which encourages co-creation of customer-centric innovation engaging internal and external stakeholders. The stakeholder engagement at par with contemporary collective intelligence overrides the conventional wisdom, inculcates community consciousness, and helps in developing change proneness among entrepreneurs. Such transformation helps entrepreneurs in restructuring business models compatible to information, communication, and marketing technology. The restructured business models can be well accommodated to e-commerce practices by adapting to technologies

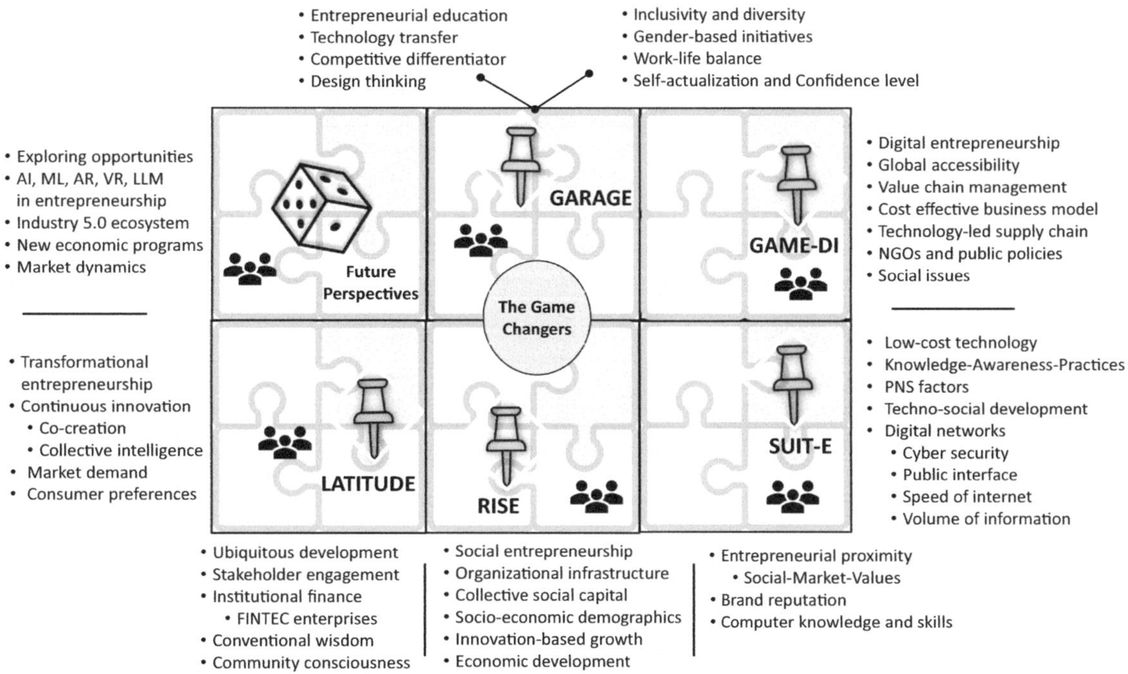

Fig. 4.1 Mapping the attributes of game changer elements (*Source* Authors)

involved in manufacturing, supply chain, and various business processes. Such restructuring of entrepreneurial business models can attract institutional finance under FINTEC programs of developing countries. The holistic effects of the above transformational elements under LATITUDE domain lead to ubiquitous development of entrepreneurship and enterprises across local areas.

As exhibited in Fig. 4.1, another set of elements comprising Revamping Innovation for Social Entrepreneurship (RISE) plays a significant role in transforming conventional entrepreneurial practices through wider social interaction by identifying the social PNS factors and creating stakeholder value. The RISE elements significantly contribute to developing social entrepreneurship in developing economies. The contribution of these elements has been witnessed by a non-governmental organization of Orissa state in India through its institution *Gram Vikas* (rural development in English), which helps entrepreneurial development at the grassroots. This institution is engaged in developing comprehensive water and sanitation system in rural areas through social enterprises by exploiting the RISE elements through interactive platforms. *Gram Vikas* educates local entrepreneurs through storytelling process with focus on the social challenges of upscaling social innovations through transformational innovation process (Chowdhury & Santos, 2013). To cater social entrepreneurship, RISE elements can be nurtured by creating collective social capital and entrepreneurial infrastructure of commons to induce innovation-based growth among entrepreneurs. The social entrepreneurship and collective innovation help in driving continuous economic development across socio-economic demographics.

SUIT-E as a game changing agent converges social ubiquity of innovation and technology in entrepreneurship, which focuses broadly on technology, knowledge, and market-led triadic entrepreneurial model. The elements of SUIT-E game changing agent emphasize in updating entrepreneurial knowledge, generating awareness about global entrepreneurship trend, and synthesizing best practices to fit to the local entrepreneurial systems. Consequently, the convergence of knowledge, awareness, and practice (KAP) helps in exploring PNS factors at grassroots to initiate low-cost technology solutions for techno-social development. The increasing advancement of information and communication technology has successfully penetrated the enterprises at the grassroots and encouraged entrepreneurs to seek benefits of digital networks. The minimum viable cyber security, transcending speed of

Internet, and volume of information transfer have significantly encouraged entrepreneurs to experience public interface to create new ideas and enrich knowledge through collective intelligence. These factors have also enhanced integrity among social, market, and value-led entrepreneurial proximity, which also helped in developing reputation of less known entrepreneurial brands. To optimize the effectiveness of SUIT-E elements, governments in most developing countries are imparting extensively the computer knowledge and skills among entrepreneurs to upgrade their know-how in technology. Along with the governments of developing countries, global corporations have also come together in promoting the technology-based local entrepreneurship. One of such experiments can be cited of HSBC Holdings, which aimed at embracing collaboration in innovation and technology ecosystem to co-create value for financing the small and medium-sized commercial clients in Asia Pacific region. This program initiated a series of open innovation program in Hong Kong to discuss various innovation initiatives. The project teams reviewed the technology performance of small and medium-sized commercial clients and their potential to resolve the local challenges through sustainable innovation. This institution analyzed the customer centricity in micro, small, and medium enterprise market to provide customer-centric solutions and develop digital enterprise systems including e-commerce platforms. The corporate partnership also encouraged business opportunities to optimize profitability under competitive conditions among FINTEC start-ups. This experiment broadly adapted the SIUT-E elements to co-create value and market for their clients (Charm & Pun, 2021).

Digitization has become one of the principal business essentials, which provides innovative opportunities to entrepreneurs to match with market-oriented and customer-centric innovation (Wibowo et al., 2023). The digital entrepreneurship stimulates entrepreneurial innovation and creative intuitions, and develop positive effects in adapting to PNS factors to innovate customer-centric products and services. The emergence of digital entrepreneurship has been a game changer to gain competitive advantages in managing the CTR factors and enhance CBP effects. The digital entrepreneurship, as an outgrowth of transcending information and communication technology, provides global accessibility to local entrepreneurs by developing cost-effective value chains and competitive business models. In this process, the role of non-governmental organizations and public policy programs of the governments in developing countries significantly contribute to generate technology awareness and market orientation to resolve embedded social issues by analyzing PNS factors effectively (e.g., Leong et al., 2022). Consequently, the ease of use of technology and perceived usefulness of low-cost and accessible technologies in entrepreneurial operations comprising computer-aided designing, robotic manufacturing, and AI-based manufacturing process support global accessibility to markets and entrepreneurship in a digital interface (GAME-DI).

The convergence of growth and acceleration in restructuring the accountable gender entrepreneurship (GARAGE) is emerging as one of the major challenges for the governments of developing countries to ensure increasing female labor force participation in economic activities to gain social empowerment. Entrepreneurial education, inclusivity and diversity, and gender-based initiatives promoted by government and non-governmental organizations are generating confidence and accountability among women entrepreneurs. The diverse entrepreneurial trades adopted by women entrepreneurs such as manufacturing fashion accessories, cosmetics, and digital printing require skill development to establish competitive differentiation among male and female entrepreneurs. To ensure such transition, governments of developing countries need to synchronize trade-specific transfer of technology with changing market ecosystem. The confidence of female entrepreneurs rises with self-actualization on contemporary entrepreneurial practices and effective work-life balance in carrying out the entrepreneurial activities independently in the society (Wang & Cheng, 2021). It is necessary to reform the social values and consciousness on the entrepreneurial activities led by women by highlighting the economic contributions of gender in household management. Therefore, increase in the income of female entrepreneurs must be considered as a bargaining power to encourage entrepreneurial growth and to accelerate the enterprise-market dynamics in local–global context (Chiappori, 1992).

Frugal innovation and low-cost technology have wider dissemination through social networks, which convey the collective intelligence and exhibit the experience on crowd behavior in analyzing the PNS factors and converge them with CTR and CBP outcomes. The social ubiquity through social networks encourages attaining new *knowledge* and technology *awareness*, and developing best *practices* (KAP) by analyzing the collective intelligence to experience higher cognitive absorption of entrepreneurial knowledge and skills. The social ubiquity of entrepreneurial KAP helps entrepreneurs to analyze collective intelligence, socialized practices, and search for best practices with differentiation to stay competitive in the marketplace. However, KAP increases user dependency on crowd resources and promotes learning about new technologies with changing behavioral scenarios (Bian & Leung, 2015). The increasing advancement of information and communication technology (ICT) has shown various ways to digitally connect entrepreneurs and stakeholders to attain new perspectives on KAP. The Facebook and Instagram are some of the popular social networks, which encourage social ubiquity in experimenting low-cost high-value innovation and technology to target to *big middle* consumers and develop customer-centric business model. Therefore, social ubiquity of innovation and technology in entrepreneurship (SU "T-E) appears to be one of the contemporary change agents to drive entrepreneurial practices digital to give stakeholders the power to care and share the contemporary entrepreneurial practices with updated KAP elements to increase proximity of entrepreneurial products to competitive markets. Often, the transformative impact of collective intelligence through social networks has far-reaching effect beyond marketing and consumer behavior. Digital networks have the potential to develop online entrepreneurial brands and foster collaboration with key partners by sharing knowledge and innovation to develop cultural, ethnic, and techno-social phenomenon on entrepreneurial products (Klier et al., 2014).

One of the growing challenges for entrepreneurs in the changing market scenarios is to reduce consumer uncertainty and increase customer value for entrepreneurial products, which have low brand equity in the market due to unfamiliar brand reputation and guaranty against value for money. The social learning through collective intelligence increases the analytical behavior among consumers to make decision towards positive or negative values associated with entrepreneurial products and services. The social ubiquity of entrepreneurial innovation and differentiated products reduces the risk of product-value mismatch and simplifies the process of buying decisions (Choi, 2020). One of the major challenges in developing digital entrepreneurship at local level is to provide the computer knowledge and skills and ensure Internet availability at the grassroots enterprises. In addition, the speed of Internet, volume of information, and cost of data consumption are the vulnerable factors associated with integrating entrepreneurs with contemporary digital networks and provide substantial security in digital sharing and learning processes.

The cyber-security concerns in developing new interfaces, sharing innovation, and building relationships with new actors require public policy support in developing economies. The high-speed digital networks, artificial intelligence, and industrial Internet-of-Things might raise significant cyber security and privacy concerns. The government regulations and cyber security interventions should come into effect to encourage digital entrepreneurship at the grassroots (Cheng et al., 2021).

In continuation to discussion on digital entrepreneurship, global accessibility to markets, and entrepreneurship in a digital interface (GAME-DI), the interplay of global value chain to develop new entrepreneurial ecosystems require major intervention. Such transformation is important for economic growth, local development, and business innovation. However, the hidden conflicts between family-based entrepreneurship and market-based entrepreneurship need to be resolved (Shane, 2000). The value chain in entrepreneurial process needs to be strengthened by synchronizing the cost-effective supply chain, manufacturing, operations, and marketing activities through the policy support of government in streamlining entrepreneurial activities. The non-governmental organizations in developing economies help local enterprises in creating integrated value chains through not-for-profit programs. There are many social issues and complex partner relationships in developing local and global value chains to achieve entrepreneurial sustainability to improve the entrepreneurial practices through continuous learning and KAP applications (Wurth et al., 2021).

Game Changer Model—LATITUDE

Rapid expansion of manufacturing and communication technology has motivated local firms to connect with global economy and changing industrial pattern in developing countries. There is a significant blend of conventional wisdom with knowledge spillover through collective intelligence and sharing of experience of multinational firms on the use and benefits of technology-led best practices. Most start-up enterprises at the grassroots develop low-cost innovation based on transmission of technologies from large firms to local markets. However, these technologies are modified according to the availability of local resources, knowledge and skills, community infrastructure, and public policy support in adapting to market-based technologies. The micro level evidence for technology based on knowledge spillovers of large firms exhibits the potential of technology-led production; however, the success of local technologies to fit to market-oriented production remains limited (Bloom et al., 2013). The domestic industries linked with local micro, small, and medium enterprises typically experience low business scaling and often face challenges in establishing their commercial brands. The major challenge faced by local enterprises in developing local area technology with low cost to ensure high performance in domestic markets has emerged as a community concern, which should be attended by the governments of developing countries through effective public policies. Innovations at micro, small, and medium enterprises are largely co-created, co-located, and co-evolved through strategic alliances with large firms within the local boundaries. The large firms, which tend to establish alliances with local enterprises, diffuse technology, manufacturing process, product designing, and marketing strategies in a consortium production model by exercising the centralized control over major technology and production operations. The transfer of technology from large firms to micro, small, and medium enterprises also encourages adoption of local innovations, which have market potential (Cen et al., 2023). Such process faces empirical challenges in converging local innovations with commercial innovations through reverse innovation approaches, which depend largely exogenous factors. Synchronizing production variabilities of local entrepreneurial ecosystem with wider market environment require restructuring of business strategies by developing commercial brands, create value for stakeholders, and ensure competitive advantages. In addition, improving innovation capacity, sharing ownership, introducing online and offline marketspace, and developing profit sharing strategies have significant intervention in enhancing the market proximity of local enterprises.

The combination of innovation, information and communication technology, and general-purpose technology (GPT) has emerged as the promising business needs to complement the changing market requirements and providing consumer convenience through technology use. GPT has emerged as a platform technology to drive continuous innovation using complementary technologies and network communication as collective intelligence (Cen et al., 2023). Embedding GPT concept in micro, small, and medium enterprises at the grassroots needs to be linked with capacity building in community entrepreneurship and technology infrastructure, and pooling local resources with shred economy principles under public policies of the governments in developing countries.

The productivity gains of innovation, information, and communication technology, and GPT have relatively long breakeven, but public policy programs on entrepreneurship, which provide subsidies on capital, materials, and operations, provide benefit to entrepreneurs to derive quick yields and manage their current revenue streams (Strohmaier & Rainer, 2016). Governments of many developing countries have devoted enormous efforts to support technology education to entrepreneurs and enable local market assistance to make frugal innovations a success and launch them as breakthroughs in the markets with wider proximity. Nurturing local area technology needs collaborative efforts with industry and society to demonstrate value-based outputs, marketing strategies, and prospective utilization of innovative products with embedded value-for-money (Aharonson & Schilling, 2016). As the entrepreneurial attributes and production processes have experienced various temporal and spatial adjustments, new technology based on geographical characteristics needs to be understood in the context of localized learning attributes related to local knowledge. The non-governmental organizations supporting entrepreneurial growth at local level should refine locally routed technologies to promote socio-economic and industrial growth in the region. Nonetheless, external knowledge brings forth global values for technologies with less local dependence. To integrate external knowledge with local entrepreneurial practices needs systematic planning and synchronization of resources, training, and process optimization. Therefore, acquiring and integrating spatial knowledge is an important consideration in building entrepreneurial capacity in contemporary technology and innovation process (Gao & Rai, 2023).

Ubiquitous development of entrepreneurship through transformation of technology to promote innovation and business in local area in developing economies is one of the principal challenges to be met by the governments of respective countries. Figure 4.2 dissects the activities of LATITUDE game changer agent into LATI and TUDE attributes comprising *local area technology and innovation* and *transformation and ubiquitous development of entrepreneurship*. The former part of the change agent (LATI) suggests entrepreneurial development agencies in developing countries to diffuse global technology and economy in local entrepreneurial areas through transfer of technology with focus on geo-economic transformation. Such public policies and programs require acquisition of external knowledge and manage conventional spillovers learned from family businesses. In addition, streamlining the collective intelligence, which is a pool of knowledge resources spread over digital networks, needs to be carried out within the community through social collaborators. Another influencing factor to promote local area technology and innovation is transfer of General-Purpose Technology (GPT) through public resources and public programs to induce innovations based on PNS factors. The business model for innovative products is developed through GPT resources by managing CTR, CBP, and minimum viable segment (MVS) through local collaborations and co-evolution.

The dissected latter half of LATITUDE game changer agent (TUDE attributes) focuses on entrepreneurial transformation process through public programs driven by government, public-private partnership, and non-governmental organizations. TUDE attributes have two subdomains consisting of technology transfer and entrepreneurship development. The entrepreneurial transformational agencies should map active local resources and infrastructure and encourage innovation collaboration through KAP attributes. Effective transfer of technology can be managed by imparting knowledge and skills among local entrepreneurs. To disseminate knowledge sharing and skill development, government and non-government organizations should strengthen the training of trainers (ToT) program. The ToT program can be implemented to mentor local entrepreneurs using network learning platforms. Skills and technology and innovation can be imparted through participatory and rapid learning methods, which encourages entrepreneurs to map local knowledge, resources, skills, and revenue streams to adapt to market-oriented manufacturing process. Another subdomain of TUDE attributes consists of entrepreneurship development, which argues on endogenous and exogenous factors associated with entrepreneurial actualization and business factors. The leadership and organizational culture largely influences entrepreneurial mindset towards adapting to changing innovation, technology, and market ecosystem. Therefore, change management in conventional entrepreneurship is one of the major organizational challenges, which thrusts cultural transformation among entrepreneurs. In managing such entrepreneurial transitions, effective leader-member exchange supported by strong transformational leadership makes a greater difference. Such leader-driven change management helps entrepreneurs in developing reverse accountability and collective decision making. The exogenous factors such as global access, enhanced knowledge,

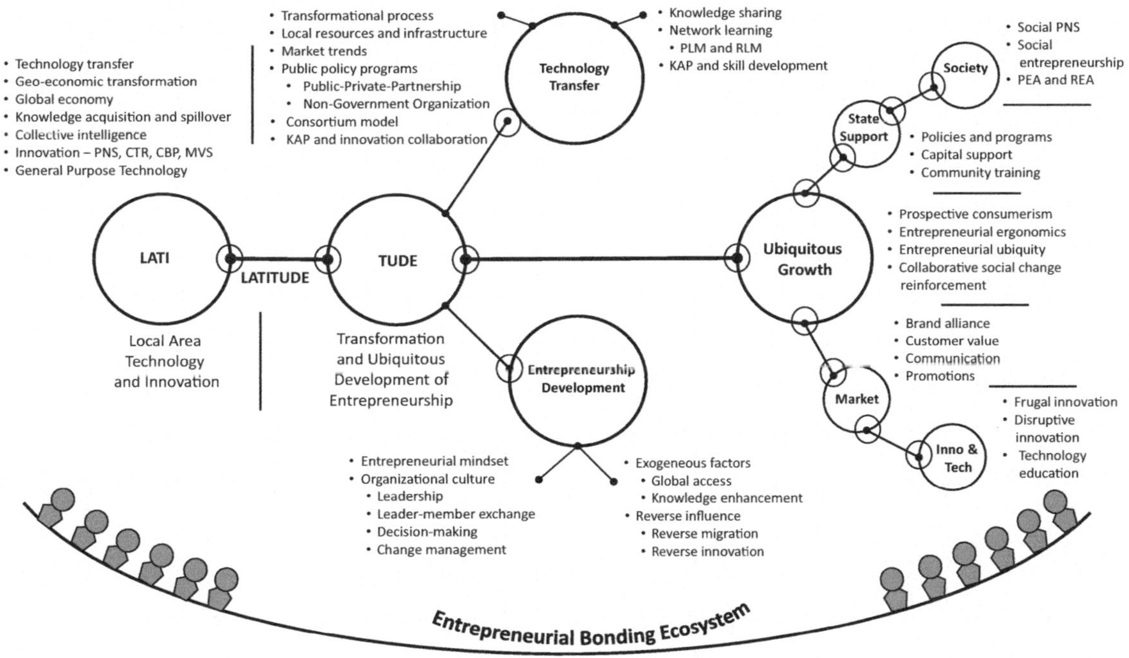

Fig. 4.2 Triadic convergence of innovation, technology, and entrepreneurial development (*Source* Authors)

and technology-led entrepreneurial processes using AI, ML, and LLM platforms help entrepreneurs in successful transition of conventional entrepreneurial practices to digital entrepreneurship. In addition, the trend of reverse migration encourages the overseas entrepreneurs and practitioners to develop enterprises in their home countries with focus on reverse innovation to benefit small-scale local innovations to grow global.

The sub-domains of ubiquitous growth of entrepreneurship include state support, societal attributes, market ecosystem, and local innovation and technology as exhibited in Fig. 4.2. The elements of ubiquitous growth of entrepreneurship at the grassroots focus on developing entrepreneurial ergonomics, which includes workplace quality, effectiveness of resource utilization, social collaboration, and value chain management to ensure managing prospective consumerism with convenient technology. In addition, reinforcement of collaborative social change through social consciousness on entrepreneurship, community leadership, and self-actualization are critical factors, which support ubiquitous growth of entrepreneurship. The government policies and programs, capital support, community training and infrastructure, and systematic entrepreneurial education within digital technology ecosystem reinforce a holistic growth of entrepreneurship. In addition, society plays a significant role in promoting entrepreneurial advancement through social entrepreneurship to identify the PNS factors by practicing Participatory Entrepreneurial Appraisal (PEA) and Rapid Entrepreneurial Appraisal (REA). PEA is a community approach in which social leaders help entrepreneurs to map available resources, capital requirement, supply chain elements, and value propositions suitable for the entrepreneurial advancement. This is a collective approach to understand the existing entrepreneurial ecosystem in local area and plan for development through community resources and infrastructure. REA is a personal approach of entrepreneurs to measure the resource availability and market transitions in the background of CTR, CBP, and MVS factors. It is a fast assessment process to know the current capability and competence level and measure the potential investments to develop market proximity and strengthen the projected revenue stream. PEA and REA attributes should align with market ecosystem to develop customer value, brand alliance, and manage advanced marketing mix elements comprising 11Ps (product, price, place, promotion, packaging, pace, people, performance, psychodynamics, posture, and proliferation). The last sub-domain of ubiquitous growth encompasses technology education and innovation taxonomy.

The most common influencing innovation types can be observed as disruptive innovation and frugal innovation, which are aligned with CTR, CBP, and MVS factors.

Local knowledge available with the entrepreneurs is commonly homogeneous, narrow, and obsolete, which requires synchronized training of contemporary technology and entrepreneurial practices to drive radical and breakthrough innovations. However, entrepreneurs at the grassroots are resilient to change management and exploit external knowledge to improve the local entrepreneurial models and create novelty in products and services through quality of innovation (Aslesen & Harirchi, 2015). Therefore, from the policy viewpoint, the governments in developing countries should build appropriate programs to converge external knowledge and technology, and market relationship to disseminate contemporary skills among entrepreneurs. The policymakers may reach out to entrepreneurial practices across geographic boundaries to develop entrepreneurial training programs to promote frugal and value-based innovations not only to support customer-centric marketing, but also to expand entrepreneurial business for industrial benefits (Peters et al., 2012).

Revamping Innovation, Growth, and Acceleration

Growth and Acceleration in Restructuring Accountable Gender Entrepreneurship (GARAGE) among micro, small, and medium enterprises depend on various explained and unexplained factors. These factors include tangible determinants such as education, finance, innovation, and technology. The intangible attributes consist of psychosocial elements, which determine the entrepreneurial set. The role of gender in local enterprises has been considered not only as social and economic concern for empowerment, but also has strong socio-political dimensions. The women entrepreneurs are largely encouraged by the social and political leaders and governments of developing countries to provide substantial capital and material resource support to nurture the growth aspirations. However, irrespective of gender, there generally exist a large number of underdog entrepreneurs who play less risk averse with high entrepreneurial growth aspirations. An increasing number of studies reveal that such underdogs have propensity for entrepreneurial growth after launching their ventures with disruptive innovations. Such entrepreneurs remain largely unknown but attribute to higher growth aspirations and business earnings by establishing prolific strategic alliances with collaborative firms (Bort & Totterman, 2023).

Acceleration of entrepreneurial activities face several challenges comprising diverse cognitive issues, socio-economic challenges such as poverty, lack of entrepreneurial education, and ability to survive in dynamic market competition. Most women entrepreneurs exhibit attributes of weak social ties, lack of finance, resilience to change, and adaptiveness to the changing innovation and technology ecosystem. These factors cause significant risk in successfully operating their enterprises besides the hardship and poverty, and embedded perceptions on risk. Entrepreneurial growth and acceleration among marginalized social groups and trades lower the prospects of economic prosperity and disrupt the systematic pattern of long-term success and growth. Consequently, the nascent enterprises often fall back of contemporary innovation and technology and succumb to their business models within niche markets. Overcoming the conventional problems in managing enterprises such as family businesses, some entrepreneurs venture innovations with high risk and develop disruptive products with challenges of commercialization. Some start-up entrepreneurs of Biomedical Engineering and Technology Innovation Center of Indian Institute of Technology, Bombay, India, penetrated medical technology market by innovating an indigenous smart stethoscope with digital functions from the conceptual stage to the functional prototype. Such disruptive product falls into the category of highly regulated industry, which is being commercialized through a systematic business model with minimum risk of failure (Chinchwadkar et al., 2017). The role of women entrepreneurship in integrating value chain in micro enterprises can be discussed as a Philippines experience of GREAT women, a brand which is an outgrowth of an entrepreneurship project—Gender Responsive Economic Action for the Transformation of Women. The women entrepreneurs associated with the GREAT women brand have been engaged in retailing organic products to up-market consumers in Manilla, Philippines. The product under this brand is marketed through ECHO stores under private entity known as Earth Life Store Supply Inc. This marketing company helped micro-producers to improve their ethnic products and link them to the market network of business owners and intermediaries. This project was also internationally funded and its success scaled-up the model as a social enterprise with no risk, better resource utilization, high funding, and business expansion (Thomas & Appasamy, 2018).

The community involvement in encouraging women entrepreneurs has been observed to be rising continuously in developing countries with social consciousness among women entrepreneurs. The philosophy of collectivism has significantly influenced the social and political leaders, which encouraged developing of public policies and programs for group-based financing and creating social infrastructure for skill development, creativity, and introducing frugal innovation in technology. Many studies endorse that micro-lending has been a suitable financing mechanism to provide working capital to micro enterprises within the social regulations of small loans, savings, and payment services. A traditional micro-savings system enabled Nigerian women to save their business during pandemic of COVID-19. This social system of micro-savings based on trust allowed women entrepreneurs to manage their business within informal economy to survive the business shutdowns. The women entrepreneurs, who are the stakeholders of this micro financing system called as *Ajo*, follow the cooperative saving culture encouraging them to contribute a portion of their savings on weekly and monthly basis to receive full amount over time to invest in their business (Simba et al., 2023).

Revamping Innovation for Social Entrepreneurship (RISE) requires stakeholder engagement in understanding underlying social problems, existing needs, and appropriate solutions through social participation. Social entrepreneurship can be developed mapping the social necessities and livelihood landscape by measuring the proximity to market, availability of resources, creativity and family business footprints, and evolution of entrepreneurial skills. Social entrepreneurship is emerging as a principal move towards sustainable development through volunteerism and civic commitment. The critical difference between social and traditional entrepreneurship can be seen in delineating the social mission and the market. Social entrepreneurs emphasize on ways to produce progressive social business or public properties (Heeks et al., 2014). Social entrepreneurship has high-value proposition intended to drive societal transformations. Such entrepreneurs address social issues and problems and empower transformational progress throughout the system. The dominant factor for the rise of social entrepreneurship is the societal pressure on green recovery and sustainability governance (Gandhi & Raina, 2018). Another successful and impactful social enterprise is ME to WE that provides Fairtrade products and global volunteer trips to a mostly millennial audience. It was launched in 2006 by two Canadian brothers and has grown rapidly. The enterprise allows consumers to enter a unique code from ME to WE products to transparently see exactly how and where the funds from their purchases are used for the needy people to transform lives by providing financial support on various vital requirement (Rajagopal, 2021a). The attributes of entrepreneurial change agent models GARAGE and RISE are exhibited in Fig. 4.3.

Growth and Acceleration in Restructuring Accountable Gender Entrepreneurship (GARAGE) is one of the principal change agents administered through government and social programs within the market dynamics and entrepreneurial strategies as discussed in Fig. 4.3. The elements of entrepreneurial transformation of GAARAGE change agent have both positive and negative dimensions, which promotes growth perspectives and affects entrepreneurial mindset due to resilience and dilemma towards change management. The GARAGE change agent supports local economic growth by accelerating entrepreneurial operations through effective resource management by mapping the available resources, accounting for pool resources, and optimizing resource utilization. This change agent model inculcates reverse accountability among entrepreneur besides social and state interventions in administering, monitoring, and evaluating the entrepreneurial economic growth process. The public programs on transfer of technology, skill development, and entrepreneurial education initiated by governments in developing countries stimulate economic growth of enterprises and empower entrepreneurs to stay competitive in the marketplace by adapting to changing innovation and technology ecosystems. Contrary to the growth perspectives, the resilience and dilemma among entrepreneurs negatively affect the transformation process of conventional enterprises as conceptualized in the garage change agent model. The resistance to change management and adaptiveness is largely driven by amateur transformational philosophy of leaders and the quality of leader-member exchange. Consequently, entrepreneurs develop low risk-taking ability and are demotivated towards global access for continuous learning. Such resilience and embedded dilemma invoke individualism in decision making as against the contemporary trend of collectivism in diffusion of knowledge and decision making.

Strategies on revamping innovation and social entrepreneurship can be developed as another set of transformational change agent models by encouraging social participation to explore PNS factors and develop skills on frugal and incremental innovations to increase the proximity of entrepreneurial products to competitive markets. To gain prominence

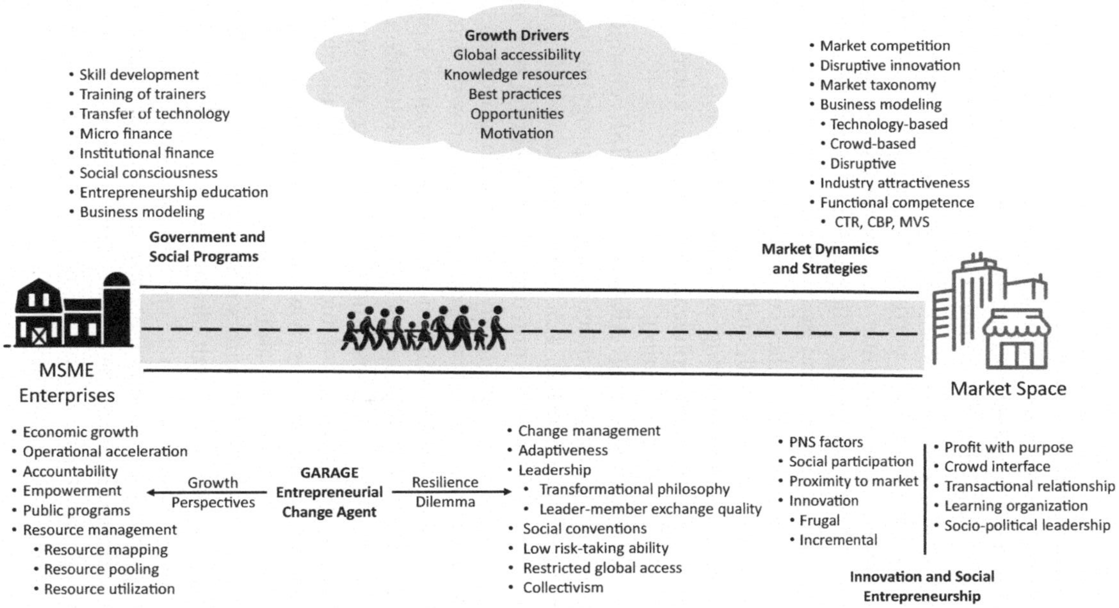

Fig. 4.3 Attributes of entrepreneurial change agents and growth drivers (*Source* Authors)

of entrepreneurial products and brands, crowd interface of entrepreneurs needs to be encouraged, which will also be helpful in disseminating the socio-economic business philosophy of *profit with purpose*. Revamping innovation in social entrepreneurship also requires strengthening transactional relationship in various client segments comprising business-to-business (B-to-B), business-to-consumers (B-to-C), consumer-to-consumer (C-to-C), and online-to-offline (O-to-O). To successfully penetrate B-to-B segment, entrepreneurs should develop strategies within business canvas by identifying key partners, key resources, distribution channels, cost structure, and revenue streams besides other elements of business canvas. The marketing efficiency in C-to-C segment can be inked with digital networks and social media channels to develop proximity among consumers in the competitive markets. To ensure continuous innovation, micro, small, and medium enterprises must grow as learning organizations emphasizing on systems thinking. Such organizational behavior requires socio-political leadership and entrepreneurial consciousness towards self-actualization.

The growth drivers moderating ARAGE and RISE change agent models are supported by the government and social programs in developing countries as illustrated in Fig. 4.3. The global accessibility, knowledge resources, application of best practices, and exploring new opportunities as key growth drivers are motivated through government and social programs. The broad effects on promotion of growth drivers are visible through the skill development and training of trainer's program aimed at effective transfer of technology, entrepreneurial education, micro financing, and competitive business modeling among entrepreneurs. These transformational change agent models help in inculcating social consciousness among entrepreneurs towards continuous learning and change to face market dynamics and develop appropriate strategies. Creative entrepreneurs benefiting with such transformational effects can survive market competition through disruptive innovation and varied business modeling (technology-based, crowd-based, and disruptive) to gain functional competence within the existing industry attractiveness. The functional competence can be achieved by minimizing the CTR effects, optimizing the CBP outputs, and refining the experience of marketing within minimum viable segments.

Traditional approaches to social enterprise strategy of both start-up enterprises and large companies assume that the social behavior and values are relatively stable and predictable. However, new technologies and greater transparency have combined to achieve the social business goals on sustainability. Such shift in the business environment has generated more risk and vulnerability among social enterprises in engaging with new innovative projects. Social enterprises that thrive to follow the integrated innovation strategies as discussed above can alter the consumer behavior quickly and manage the market demand. These enterprises experiment rapidly and frequently with products and services as well as business models, processes, and strategies, to achieve a sustainable market for innovative product. Innovation entrepreneurship is a convergence of start-up enterprises and the sponsoring companies, which moves from the stage of initiation to the systematic project management to commercialization, and finally developing sustainable innovation through incremental innovations (Rajagopal, 2021a). Social entrepreneurship requires strong moral engagement with self-regulatory processes associated with community welfare measures with fair engagement of stakeholders. The social entrepreneur should have cognitive justification to introspect as a good person to contribute to the welfare of the society orchestrating resources and overcoming the grey areas in public projects, which affect the potential social benefits (Muldoon et al., 2022). Social innovation has been conceptualized as crowd-based interface to meet various challenges embedded in the society through stakeholder participation. Social innovation is supportive to government programs intended to solve environmental and social challenges to help sustainable development. The effective transformation of social entrepreneurship needs intervention of socio-political leadership and capabilities to implement social change and revitalize conventional-social aspects through a paradigm shift. In this process, social entrepreneurs should be empowered in reconfiguring social goals, practices, and collective actions by utilizing the available economic resources (Grilo & Moreira, 2022).

Social entrepreneurship exhibits a hierarchy between socially conscious entrepreneurs at one end and beneficiaries at the other end to develop transactional relationship and transform the social benefits. This implies a differentiation between knowing the social needs, empowering entrepreneurs, and bringing in the passive beneficiaries to share benefits of social entrepreneurship. Ideally, social entrepreneurship influences potentially overshadowed social needs and reconstructs interaction between entrepreneurs and beneficiaries. Therefore, social entrepreneurship has been considered as a tool for generating social value and promoting economic development based on the voice of stakeholders. It aligns the archetypical roles of entrepreneurs, beneficiaries, and socio-political leaders by developing value-based relationship exploring individual and collective experiences (Berglund & Schwartz, 2013). Small innovation-led firms grow as learning organizations. They become inspirational, energetic places to work, where even relationships with customers and suppliers improve. However, a more integrated view will enable companies to innovate for long-term profitability and sustainability. There are three core competencies that learning organizations must master to profit from sustainability: encourage systemic thinking; convene strategic market players and customers towards changing conventional thinking; and take the lead in reshaping economic, political, and societal forces that baffle change (Senge & Carstedt, 2001). The social entrepreneurs are actively engaged in sustainability-driven business projects within the emerging concepts of circular economy. A company, which has grown over the years within the retail industry in manufacturing housewares and personal care consumer goods in a niche market, has developed business model on recycling plastics of 5th stage. This enterprise based in Massachusetts has developed purpose-driven social enterprise model to meet the sustainability challenge and generate social benefits as a value addition to its corporate reputation. This enterprise has focused its business model on SEERS framework comprising Social, Environmental, Economic Responsibility and Sustainability-based values. This enterprise extensively engages stakeholders to create and implement social innovations, which are pre-identified with focus on social and economic value generation (Erzurumlu, 2018).

Social Ubiquity, Global Accessibility, and Technology in Entrepreneurship

Social Ubiquity of Innovation and Technology in Entrepreneurship (SUIT-E) is a broad challenge in developing countries, which needs to inculcate entrepreneurial consciousness about use of innovation and technology for social and economic development at the grassroots. The core elements in developing social ubiquity through social entrepreneurship need to converge diverse factors like stakeholders' expectations, societal needs, low-cost innovation and technology, macroeconomic factors, sustainability, and enterprise management approaches. Crowdsourcing or collective intelligence has emerged as a dynamic tool in the business ecosystem today, which is supported by the stakeholders. They support companies in co-creation and co-evolution process with stakeholders through social interaction, social innovations, and social governance. Business ecosystems linked with the sustainability goals drive public-private entrepreneurship (collaborations) to meet the sustainable development goals through social- and frugal innovations. Taxonomy of leadership and employee engagement largely drive the corporate governance practices as central to the business ecosystem. Among various subsystems associated with the core business ecosystems, stakeholders are influenced by the cognitive subsystem comprising perceptions, emotions, and social interactions. Social and innovation subsystems include social values, entrepreneurship education, and utilitarian innovations. Management of resources and factors of production, procurement, and transactions of public goods constitute some significant factors of macroeconomic subsystem (Rajagopal, 2021a). Alike other change agent models SUIT-E and GAME-DI entrepreneurial transformational models can also play significant role in entrepreneurial transformational process as illustrated in Fig. 4.4.

Managing social ubiquity of innovation and technology in entrepreneurship (SUIT-E) is a major challenge for both social and government organizations in developing countries due to entrepreneurial resilience to change. Therefore, government and non-governmental organizations need to diligently engage in developing entrepreneurial consciousness towards market- and technology-led transformation. In this process, the major challenge is to encourage stakeholder engagement on functional roles and manage predetermined expectations. Effective knowledge sharing through corporate experience, best practices, and collective intelligence induces entrepreneurs in developing ambidextrous social innovation with industrial and consumption purposes. Elements of GAME-DI model propose entrepreneurial agility through interactive functions, collective decisions, and flexible implementation of digital entrepreneurship and e-commerce strategies by optimizing e-commerce strategies. The technology-led business practices guide entrepreneurs in making optimal use of social media platforms to enhance the speed of their business, stay competitive, and diversify entrepreneurial trade streams. The general conditions of micro, small, and medium enterprises encompass low capital, conventional wisdom, and limited scope of incremental innovation. These enterprises largely grow out of family business with local stakeholders with low-cost entrepreneurship practices. Consequently, these enterprises operate in niche market. The entrepreneurial

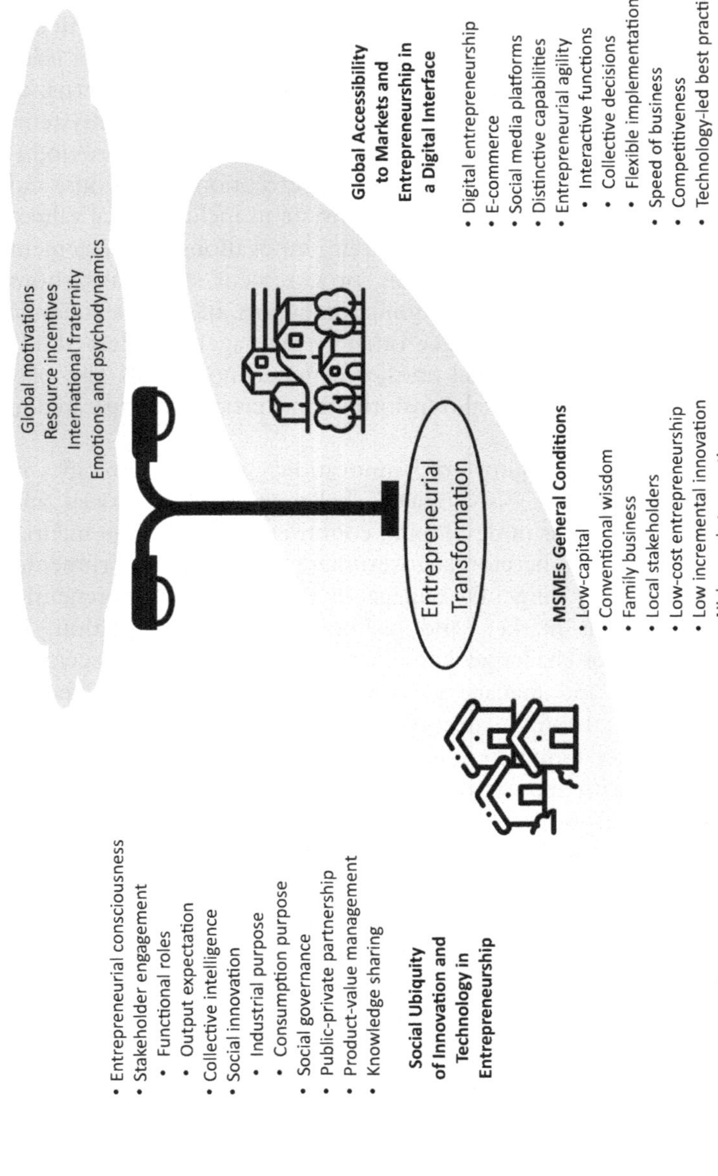

Fig. 4.4 Entrepreneurial transformation through innovation and technology interface (*Source* Authors)

transformation, therefore, has become a global concern. Global motivation and local resource incentives are encouraged by the international fraternity to support entrepreneurial emotions and psychodynamics to break conventional impediments and proceed with transformational change.

The innovation subsystem within the broad business ecosystem is built upon the knowledge of stakeholders in creating and sharing their experiences across companies. In addition, knowledge institutions, policy regimes, business enterprises, and industry boundaries also contribute to the innovation subsystem. Public policies and government play an important role in promoting local innovation and forming innovation ecosystem to support social and entrepreneurial business models (Ma et al., 2019). End-users contribute to the innovation processes by contributing to the design perspectives and stimulating demand of the innovative product. Thus, stakeholders, corporate managers, and policymakers remain apprehensive about the potential of end-users driving entrepreneurial innovation (Nielsen, 2020). The role of frugal innovations on sustainability needs, their branding and marketing strategies, and product-value management are also addressed in this chapter. This chapter emphasizes the external and internal factors that help companies in implementing environment-friendly business activities and developing green capabilities with retailers, service providers, and civic bodies. However, profits earned on frugal innovations are much lower than high-value high-technology innovative products targeted to the up-front or premier markets. The user-driven innovation conforms to the consumers' needs and would help them realize its value at relatively lower costs. Accordingly, firms can 'refresh' innovation policy to embrace user-driven innovation and encouraging user-driven innovation against high-cost-complex market innovations (Martin & Milway, 2012).

Global Accessibility to Markets and Entrepreneurship in a Digital Interface (GAME-DI) is often challenging for start-up entrepreneurs due to lack of adequate technological capabilities and competence, and resources for operating on digital platforms. However, the low-cost options for creating new e-commerce platforms are available on community Web hosting services in many developing countries. Amid growing information and communication technology, firms are recognizing the power of the Internet as a platform for co-creating value with customers. Internet has impacted the process of collaborative innovation as a key process in value co-creation. Distinctive capabilities of the Internet as a platform for customer engagement including interactivity, enhanced reach, persistence, speed, and flexibility suggest that firms can use these capabilities to engage customers in collaborative product innovation through a variety of Internet-based mechanisms. The network mechanisms can facilitate collaborative innovation at different stages of the new product development process (back end vs. front end stages) and for differing levels of customer involvement (high reach vs. high richness). As the competition is increasing in the global marketplace, most firms are reorienting their marketing communication strategies through customer-to-customer networking as the customer-driven communication is found more trustworthy and decisive. Consequently, consumers are adopting increasingly active roles in co-creating marketing communication with companies and their respective brands. Most of the emerging firms are working hard in developing online social marketing programs and brand campaigns to reach consumers where they 'live' virtually. However, the challenge faced by many companies is apparently the way to be active in social media, as most firms do not have clear understanding of how to manage the social networks effectively, and what performance indicators they should be measuring and how. Further, as companies develop social media strategies, platforms such as YouTube, Facebook, and Twitter are too often treated as stand-alone elements rather than the part of an integrated system. The collaboration and networking platforms empower employees, customers, and partners to be active participants in the global conversation. Social media tools and platforms provide an effective communications channel for the customer-centric business communication and as a transparent knowledge sharing initiative across the organization. Firms must establish a process for delivering the voice of truth through right communication in social media platforms by disseminating authentic, trusted, and believable information. This reinforces the idea that social media can be promoted by the firms as a tool not only to voice ideas and concerns, but also to get accurate and credible solutions on various issues of consumers (Rajagopal, 2021b).

References

Aharonson, B. S., & Schilling, M. A. (2016). Mapping the technological landscape: Measuring technology distance, technological footprints, and technology evolution. *Research Policy, 45*(1), 81–96.

Aslesen, H. W., & Harirchi, G. (2015). The effect of local and global linkages on the innovativeness in ICT SMEs: Does location-specific context matter? *Entrepreneurship and Regional Development, 27*, 644–669.

Berglund, K., & Schwartz, K. (2013). Holding on the anomaly of social entrepreneurship: Solving dilemmas and dealing with disharmonies. *Journal of Social Entrepreneurship, 4*(3), 237–255.

Bian, M., & Leung, L. (2015). Linking loneliness, shyness, smartphone addiction symptoms, and patterns of smartphone use to social capital. *Social Science Computer Review, 33*(1), 61–79.

Bloom, N., Schankerman, M., & Van Reenen, J. (2013). Identifying technology spillovers and product market rivalry. *Econometrica, 81*(4), 1347–1393.

Bort, J., & Totterman, H. (2023). The growth aspirations of underdog entrepreneurs. *Journal of Business Research, 165*. https://doi.org/10.1016/j.jbusres.2023.114055

Charm, T., & Pun, H. (2021, November). HSBC: Embracing open innovation for SMEs. *Harvard Business School Publishing*, 1–15.

Cen, J., Fu, F., Yang, Y., Yan, J., & Li, J. (2023). Distant or local? The roles of knowledge search on general purpose technology innovation in emerging industries. *Journal of Innovation & Knowledge, 8*(2). https://doi.org/10.1016/j.jik.2023.100331

Cheng, L. -K., Huang, H. -K., & Yang, S. -Y. (2021). Attitude toward 5G: The moderating effect of regulatory focus. *Technology in Society, 67*. https://doi.org/10.1016/j.techsoc.2021.101795

Chiappori, P. A. (1992). Collective labor supply and welfare. *Journal of Political Economy, 100*(3), 437–467.

Chinchwadkar, R., Ahmed, M., & Pratap, S. (2017). *BETIC, IIT Bombay: Commercializing a novel digital stethoscope*. Harvard Business School Publishing.

Choi, J. (2020). How consumers engage in & utilize the source of electronic word-of-mouth (e-WOM)? *Academy of Strategic Management Journal, 19*(2), 1–12.

Chowdhury, I., & Santos, F. (2013). Gram Vikas: What is the essence of social entrepreneurship? *Harvard Business School Publishing*, 1–22.

Erzurumlu, S. (2018). *Preserve: Growing a sustainable consumer goods company*. Harvard Business School Publishing.

Frederiks, A. J., Englis, B. G., Ehrenhard, M. L., & Groen, A. J. (2019). Entrepreneurial cognition and the quality of new venture ideas: An experimental approach to comparing future-oriented cognitive processes. *Journal of Business Venture, 34*(2), 327–347.

Gandhi, T., & Raina, R. (2018). Social entrepreneurship: The need, relevance, facets and constraints. *Journal of Global Entrepreneurship Research, 8*(9), 1–13. https://doi.org/10.1186/s40497-018-0094-6

Gao, X., & Rai, V. (2023). Knowledge acquisition and innovation quality: The moderating role of geographical characteristics of technology. *Technovation, 125*. https://doi.org/10.1016/j.technovation.2023.102766

Grilo, R., & Moreira, A. C. (2022). The social as the heart of social innovation and social entrepreneurship: An emerging area or an old crossroads? *International Journal of Innovation Studies, 6*(2), 53–66.

Guzman, J., & Kacperczyk, A. (2019). Gender gap in entrepreneurship. *Research Policy, 48*(7), 1666–1680.

Heeks, R., Foster, C., & Nugroho, Y. (2014). New models of inclusive innovation for development. *Innovation and Development, 4*(2), 175–185.

Kamran, S. M., Khaskhely, M. K., Nassani, A. A., Haffar, M., & Abro, M. M. Q. (2022). Social entrepreneurship opportunities via distant socialization and social value creation. *Sustainability, 14*(6), 1–25.

Kier, A. S., & McMullen, J. S. (2018). Entrepreneurial imaginativeness in new venture ideation. *Academy of Management Journal, 61*(6), 2265–2295.

Kier, A. S., & McMullen, J. S. (2020). Entrepreneurial imaginativeness and new venture ideation in newly forming teams. *Journal of Business Venturing, 35*(6). https://doi.org/10.1016/j.jbusvent.2020.106048

Klier, J., Klier, M., & Wigand, R. T. (2014). The connectedness, pervasiveness and ubiquity of online social networks. *Computer Networks, 75*, 473–476.

Leong, C., Tan, F. T. C., Tan, B., & Faisal, F. (2022). The emancipatory potential of digital entrepreneurship: A study of financial technology-driven inclusive growth. *Information & Management, 59*(3), Article 103384.

Ma, L., Liu, Z., Huang, X., & Li, T. (2019). The impact of local government policy on innovation ecosystem in knowledge resource scarce region: Case study of Changzhou, China. *Science, Technology and Society, 24*(1), 29–52.

Mair, J., & Schoen, O. (2007). Successful social entrepreneurial business models in the context of developing economies: An explorative study. *International Journal of Emerging Markets, 2*(1), 54–68.

Martin, R., & Milway, J. (2012, September). *User-driven innovation: Putting an end to inventing in the dark* (Working paper). Rotman School of Management.

McMullen, J. S. (2015). Entrepreneurial judgment as empathic accuracy: A sequential decision-making approach to entrepreneurial action. *Journal of Institutional Economics, 11*(3), 651–681.

Mmbaga, N. A., Mathias, B. D., Williams, D. W., & Cardon, M. S. (2020). A review of and future agenda for research on identity in entrepreneurship. *Journal of Business Venture, 35*, Article 106049. https://doi.org/10.1016/j.jbusvent.2020.106049

Muldoon, J., Davis, P. E., Bendickson, J. S., McDowell, W. C., & Liguori, E. W. (2022). Paved with good intentions: Moral disengagement and social entrepreneurship. *Journal of Innovation & Knowledge, 7*(4). https://doi.org/10.1016/j.jik.2022.100237

Nielsen, K. R. (2020). Policymakers' views on sustainable end-user innovation: Implications for sustainable innovation. *Journal of Cleaner Production, 254*. https://doi.org/10.1016/j.jclepro.2020.120030

Peters, M., Schneider, M., Griesshaber, T., & Hoffmann, V. H. (2012). The impact of technology-push and demand-pull policies on technical change—Does the locus of policies matter? *Research Policy, 41*, 1296–1308.

Rajagopal. (2021a). *Sustainable businesses in developing economies—Socio-economic and governance perspectives*. Palgrave Macmillan.

Rajagopal. (2021b). *Crowd-Based business models—Using collective intelligence for market competitiveness*. Palgrave Macmillan.

Sarasvathy, S. D. (2021). The middle class of business: Endurance as a dependent variable in entrepreneurship. *Entrepreneurship Theory and Practice, 45*(5), 1054–1082.

Senge, P. M., & Carstedt, G. (2001). Innovating our way to next industrial revolution. *MIT Sloan Management Review, 42*(2), 24–38.

Shane, S. (2000). Prior knowledge and the discovery of entrepreneurial opportunities. *Organizational Science, 11*(4), 448–469.

Simba, A., Ogundana, O. M., Braune, E., & Dana, L.-P. (2023). Community financing in entrepreneurship: A focus on women entrepreneurs in the developing world. *Journal of Business Research, 163*. https://doi.org/10.1016/j.jbusres.2023.113962

Strohmaier, R., & Rainer, A. (2016). Studying general purpose technologies in a multi-sector framework: The case of ICT in Denmark. *Structural Change and Economic Dynamics, 36*, 34–49.

Thomas, H., & Appasamy, L. (2018). *Great women: Integrating micro-entrepreneurs into the regional value chain*. Harvard Business School Publishing,

Wang, H., & Cheng, Z. (2021). Mama loves you: The gender wage gap and expenditure on children's education in China. *Journal of Economic Behavior & Organization, 188*, 1015–1034.

Wibowo, A., Narmaditya, B., Suparno, S., Dianta, K., Sebayang, A., Mukhtar, S., Hakimi, M., & Shafiai, M. (2023). How does digital entrepreneurship education promote entrepreneurial intention? The role of social media and entrepreneurial intuition. *Social Sciences & Humanities Open, 8*(1). https://doi.org/10.1016/j.ssaho.2023.100681

Wurth, B., Stam, E., & Spigel, B. (2021). Toward an entrepreneurial ecosystem research program. *Entrepreneurship Theory and Practice, 46*(3), 729–778.

PART III

The Synergy

CHAPTER 5

Synchronizing Transitional Pace

Abstract This chapter synchronizes the entrepreneurial transformation and change management models discussed in the previous chapters (Chapters 1–4). The transcending innovation and technology, and rapidly changing market behavior requires entrepreneurial alignment through effective transformation. In this process, the resource-based enterprises stay ahead of large number of micro, small, and medium enterprises due to their limited resources and managerial capabilities. Based on the discussions on game changer models, game analytics, and their contextual relationship with entrepreneurship, this chapter deliberates ways to synchronize the entrepreneurial transitional pace. Accordingly, the transformational synergy across innovation, technology, market, and entrepreneurial growth has been discussed by converging the divergent transformational factors. In addition, the contributions of changing public policies and political ideologies to transformational entrepreneurship in developing economies also constitute the core discussion in this chapter. Future perspective on entrepreneurial transformation in the context of technology transfer, collective intelligence, and hybrid enterprises has also been discussed in this chapter.

Keywords Transformational synergy · Entrepreneurial transition · Convergence · Future perspectives

Rajagopal and A. Rajagopal, *Unmasking Invisible Challenges in Entrepreneurship*, Palgrave Studies of Entrepreneurship and Social Challenges in Developing Economies,
https://doi.org/10.1007/978-3-031-63653-0_5

Drawing the synergy from the previous chapters across two modules comprising the need for entrepreneurial transformation, and the discussion on the elements of the game changer models, the synthesis on entrepreneurial transformation has been discussed in this chapter by convergence of divergent transformational factors and the philosophy of knowing-doing-being. The perspectives of developing hybrid enterprises through technology consortium and conscious consumerism have also been discussed in this chapter. In addition, the contributions of changing public policies and political ideologies to transformational entrepreneurship in developing economies also constitute the core discussion in this chapter.

Transformational Synergy

Entrepreneurship today is leaning heavily towards commercialization than embodying social, cultural, and anthropological perspectives. Consequently, the trends towards innovative products and creative entrepreneurial tasks in the market determine the growth of entrepreneurship. The latent demand, underneath innovations, and shadowed competitive strategies often act as game changers, which discreetly affects entrepreneurship and its business growth. Unmasking the above hidden elements has been a major challenge for entrepreneurs, social institutions, and public policy implementers. In the process of commercializing local entrepreneurship, the influence of market has been observed significantly in changing the entrepreneurship competency to attract utilitarian innovation as the key agent for entrepreneurial returns and growth continuum. To get along with market trends, the entrepreneurial dimensions have widened from singular entrepreneurship to entrepreneurial group management leading to consortium entrepreneurship. Such integrated entrepreneurial approach has both social and economic implications in managing returns, risk, and recovery through collective operations. The consortium entrepreneurship enhances operational protection and scaling of business through resource seeking and marketing management strategies. Consequently, entrepreneurship today is built around the tripartite interaction theory integrating society, business, and entrepreneurship. Social institutions in association with the current market trends help entrepreneurs in developing competitive design thinking and lean entrepreneurial management to achieve sustainable development (Ratten & Jones, 2021). Global awareness on conscious consumption has increased the demand for environmentally friendly products across countries. Consequently, consumer preferences have shifted towards green products and eco-friendly markets. Entrepreneurs are cautious about developing market-led sustainable enterprises to cater to social and market needs. However, the concept of sustainable entrepreneurship needs to be converged with market orientation by improving the capabilities and competencies of entrepreneurial practices within the changing economic and technological complexities (Gupta & Dharwal, 2022).

Contemporary entrepreneurial management involves stakeholders' engagement to coordinate with market-design goals and strategies at four levels of entrepreneurship planning comprising international, national, regional, and local levels. Such multilayered entrepreneurial coordination requires competency to unveil the underlying deepest and invisible attributes of entrepreneurship. These attributes are bundled in individual traits, hidden value systems, changing market preferences, and rapid growth of innovation and technology. To manage these divergent factors, entrepreneurs need to rebuild confidence, risk-taking behavior, and internal locus of control to match with the changing market preferences, competitiveness, and innovation (Vodă & Florea, 2019). Entrepreneurship and small start-up firms have emerged as key engines to stimulate the market through co-creation and innovation to contribute to economic growth in the region. Accordingly, the entrepreneurship is subjected to the growth alongside the market vulnerability with a major challenge to create economic opportunities and strengthen the entrepreneurial venture amid turbulence (Wellalage & Fernandez, 2019). The changing entrepreneurial philosophy encourages entrepreneurs to develop market-based designs in manufacturing, marketing, supply chain, innovations, and technology management. Enterprises that develop change absorption capabilities sustain in changing market environment and enhance customer engagement to reinforce value-driven business goals in entrepreneurship. Entrepreneurs in developing economies lean towards working with low-cost sustainability projects, though they face restricted outreach to stakeholders. Sustainability has emerged as a megatrend for businesses in the twenty-first century. Companies plan transformative changes in the organization to create social values across the competitive marketplace (Galindo & Méndez-Picazo, 2013). Achieving entrepreneurial synergy in dynamic market environment is a complex process, which involves diverse functional elements. These attributes in the context of government and social institutions, and international agencies are illustrated in Fig. 5.1.

The BEST domains, which intervene in major entrepreneurial operations to develop synergy in entrepreneurship and strengthen the business, economic, and social relationship, are exhibited in Fig. 5.1. The element of BEST domain consists of appropriate *business appraisal*, factors of *economic transition*, desired *social engagement*, and developing adequate *transactional competence*. It is necessary for micro, small, and medium enterprises irrespective of their size and volume of business transactions to conduct periodical business appraisal to measure the extent of creativity, design thinking, and streamlined competitive strategies. Such appraisal of these critical elements will help enterprises in developing collective bargaining in competitive marketplace by creating competitiveness on fundamental marketing-mix (product, price, place, and promotion). Successful management of these critical factors will lead enterprises to expand their proximity to market. In addition, periodic business appraisal helps enterprises to determine appropriate operational strategies such as lean management. Lean entrepreneurs tend to produce minimum viable products for distribution within the minimum viable segments, which ensures low CTR effects and high CBP outcomes. Lean entrepreneurship demonstrates the linear product manufacturing, processing, and marketing path, which is tested and user reviewed to determine its quality and value. Such lean entrepreneurship practice can be followed as an iterative loop to develop holistic effect in entrepreneurship by using the acquired and experiential learning to lead strategic entrepreneurial success. Business appraisal also helps in shortening the innovation and new product development cycles and tests its economic viability and technological feasibility.

The economic transition in entrepreneurial practices is affected by various global and local factors as illustrated in Fig. 5.1. Increasing global awareness about entrepreneurial practices stimulates engaging the enterprises in strategic alliances with large firms to improve production, distribution, technology use, and resource management. Fund raising through crowdfunding and public equities by projecting the growth of enterprise with strategic alliances improves the status of venture capital. Growing urbanization and smart-city ecosystems significantly contributes to the economic transition of enterprise. The public policy and programs, and sustainable practices of micro, small, and medium enterprises also

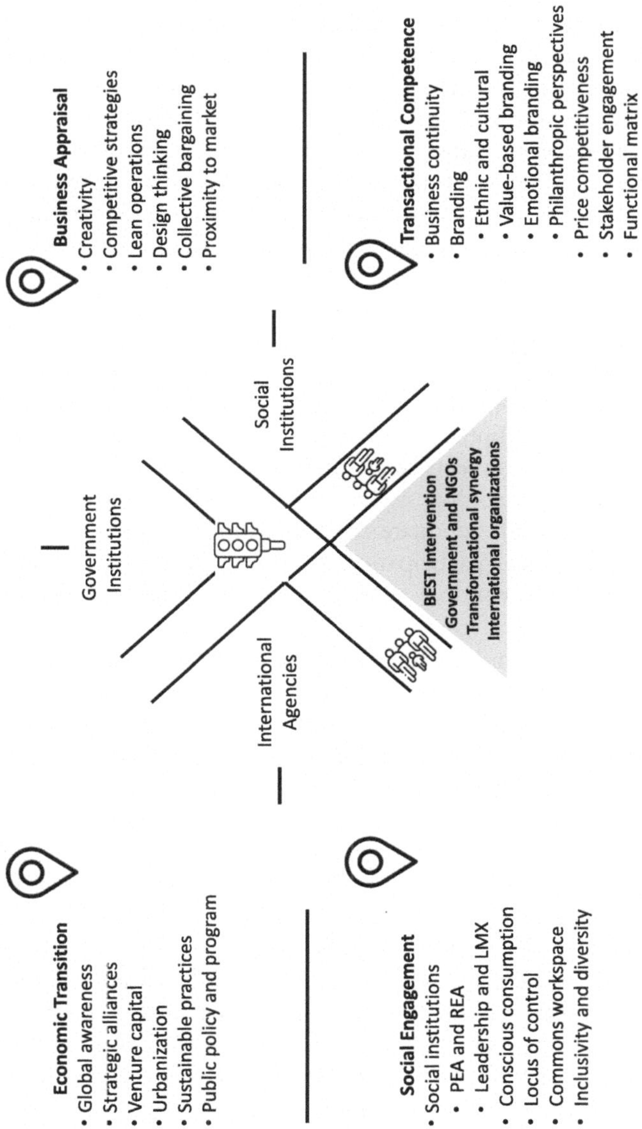

Fig. 5.1 BEST attributes and entrepreneurial synergy (*Source* Authors)

contribute to manage the smooth economic transition of these enterprises. The social engagement promotes local enterprises through participatory entrepreneurial appraisal (PEA) and rapid entrepreneurial appraisal (REA). The locus of enterprise control within social ecosystem helps in effectively managing inclusivity and diversity in enterprises and provides a common workspace to create integrity in working. The business appraisal also helps in monitoring transactional competence in maintaining business continuity and functional matrix of critical elements including CTR, CBP, and MVS to develop competitiveness in business across the basic marketing-mix elements. Entrepreneurs need to develop brands using broad criteria of ethnic and cultural attributes, value-based perceptions, emotional branding, and philanthropic perspectives. The stakeholder engagement in building entrepreneurial brands contributes to improving transactional competence.

It can be viewed from the above discussion that the intervention of BEST domain contributes to transformation of conventional enterprises successfully and connects local enterprises to competitive marketplace. Nonetheless, developing synergy to transform micro, small, and medium enterprises needs adequate support from government programs in developing countries, participation of non-governmental organizations (NGOs) and international agencies through collaboration of local government.

Advancement of technology and urbanization has induced the migration of entrepreneurs from rural to urban areas in search of better markets for their products. Such transition is demanding thorough change in entrepreneurial models to transform business with proximity to changing business ecosystem led by technology, which draws visual and tangible attractions to innovative entrepreneurial products. Consequently, value creation, value capture, and value delivery have emerged as critical factors for market proximity and entrepreneurial centricity to consumers (Czubala et al., 2022). The creation of new entrepreneurial business designs with focus on markets, society, and values contributes to economic growth and entrepreneurship. It is argued that entrepreneurial companies significantly support innovation and sustainable development meeting the challenges of changing customer preferences and social values. Entrepreneurial consortium consisting of micro-entrepreneurial companies in developing economies is collectively organized in marketing activities. Such companies in the niche pragmatically design and implement innovation and marketing programs by using public and private resources to generate social entrepreneurial products (Harsanto et al., 2022). These companies have consistently generated significant growth rates and profit margins with the sustainability programs irrespective of their size and destination. The pursuit of sustainability, therefore, has emerged as a powerful path to grow business enterprises with social values.

Micro enterprises, which are unable to ensure profit because of low investment and technological resources, often fail to seek prolific business activities. The hybrid organizations largely depend on open innovation, which is a simple way to overcome most of the personalized problems such as design thinking, pooling of resources, and managerial backdrops. The social and economic potential spanning demographic and entrepreneurial domains in the society have been identified as the bottom of the pyramid of the development perspectives (Brugmann & Prahalad, 2007). This philosophy gained increasing importance in the social entrepreneurship and inclusive innovation driven by women entrepreneurs who pioneered small-scale innovations within domestic economic field (Battilana & Lee, 2014). Consequently, entrepreneurship has become an integrated part of socio-economic and sustainable development model despite paucity of resources, local criticism, and adverse implementation of public policies in developing economies. Such difficulties have included entrepreneurship inherently with market-oriented growth, technology-driven managerial competence, and competitive vulnerability. This situation drives entrepreneurship at the grassroots of transformational change and overcome various institutional spheres of resource management, use of technology, proximity-to-market, and upstream growth (Ahl & Marlow, 2012).

Convergence of Transformational Factors

The global market trends of innovative entrepreneurial products are largely supported by digital marketing embedding visualization and digital diffusion of communication among various market players including potential customers. In this process, the socio-psychological factors like emotions, experience, and ecstasy to adapt to entrepreneurial products play a significant role and differentiate the uncommon innovations. The changing consumer preferences towards having the less known products as fashion icons are becoming a face in the niche. This marketing philosophy is significantly supported by the global fashion trends alongside the industry 4.0 revolution to integrate technology and local entrepreneurship. Local entrepreneurship has emerged as low-cost innovation for utilitarian products, which enables masses not only to participate as potential customers, but also to serve as co-creators, suppliers, and producers. Therefore, local entrepreneurship focused on utilitarian products and inculcating social consciousness are considered as the key source of economic open innovation and business growth. These entrepreneurs are active social agents, who gather weight in crowdsourced innovations, social capital formation, and deriving business models from social networks.

The previous chapters emphasize on five critical game changer models linking local area transfer of technology to revamp innovation for social entrepreneurship for growth and acceleration, social ubiquity, and global accessibility of markets to entrepreneurship in a digital interface. Developing local area technology within the proximity of entrepreneurs and social ecosystem is one of the emerging challenges to provide cost-effective entrepreneurial growth. Innovation in local enterprises largely depends on the transfer of technology leading to business transformation and overall economic growth of enterprises (Fontana, 2007). Evolving utilitarian technology markets in local enterprises not only offer a cost-effective market proposition, but also attract a great deal of attention as the new product innovations often create market continuum for utilitarian products. This requires a dynamic and skill-sensitive technology transfer environment to encourage entrepreneurs to continue with adaptation of changing technology and market ecosystem. However, transformation of local enterprises through transfer of technology and ubiquitous development of entrepreneurship has emerged as the joint responsibility of industry and local government. These factors are explained in the model LATITUDE as one of the game changers in developing entrepreneurship by converging the social and economic challenges at the grassroots.

Restructuring gender perspectives in entrepreneurship and integrating the entrepreneurial development with the social and economic factors of growth and teceleration (technology-led entrepreneurial acceleration) are becoming increasingly important in developing economies. Women entrepreneurs are becoming central to social and economic growth that requires sustainability and accountability despite public policy support and community dynamics. The transfer of technology to women entrepreneurs can be effective in a 6A model comprising Awareness (technology information), Attributes (markets and consumers), Association (consortium), Acquisition (low-cost innovation and technology), Appraisal (design thinking and marketability), and Alignment (empowerment, accountability, and responsiveness). The GARAGE model discusses the growth and acceleration in gender-based entrepreneurship to restructure entrepreneurial development process and growth using the 6A approach (Rajagopal, 2023). The social and economic transformation at the bottom of the pyramid is shifting rapidly with the changing social and industrial development led by advancement in technology, changing PNS factors, and relationship between the society and firms. The bottom line of enterprises grounded on social and ethnic foundations is facing challenges to compete with aggressive innovation technology and manufacturing. The social consciousness among local enterprises to adapt to new technologies and business models is yet to evolve and emerge as disruptive enterprises with breakthrough solutions in competitive markets and polarize consumers towards less known brands. Therefore, the concept of advancement of people's actions and responsive technologies is critical to entrepreneurial development by integrating *research* (challenge-based), *innovation* (low-cost and incremental), sustainability (green consumption), and *entrepreneurship* (micro, small, and medium enterprises) to create and enhance socio-economic values of entrepreneurship. These factors are discussed in the RISE paradigm with the perspective of revamping innovation for social entrepreneurship (Molina & Rajagopal, 2023).

The SUIT-E model in the book discusses social omnipresence in innovation and technology adapted to both social and market-based entrepreneurial ecosystem. The social ubiquity provides collective perceptions to entrepreneurs to help in understanding voice of customers, identifying critical-to-quality elements, and appropriately managing the quality function deployment in the innovation and technology-led entrepreneurial projects. The social consciousness and consensus encourage entrepreneurs to adapt to just do it and just feel right notions to implement in practice. Accordingly, the SUIT-E model paves passage from community to niche and niche to open market through value-based governance and grapevine effect. The GAME-DI is an upstream market model, which integrates global accessibility to markets and entrepreneurship. Entrepreneurial products developed with low-cost innovation and technology with high utilitarian value can reach global markets and establish their brands in alliance with pre-identified corporate patronage. The

GAME-DI model also integrates the functionality of reverse innovation and reverse accountability in developing technology-led products for global markets. The electrocardiogram machine GE MAC-400/800 of General Electric Company is an example of reverse innovation. However, such reverse innovation process did not adhere to reverse accountability, digital interface, and hybridity to support both global and local markets.

The convergence of game changing factors in local enterprises influences the entrepreneurial transformation process by converging global trends, innovation, and technology. Transforming global trends and the impact of industry 4.0 on digitization of entrepreneurial firms leads to increase in market competitiveness. The advancement of information and communication technology penetrated through the social media channels has significantly activated crowd cognition and collective intelligence as a radical game changer in local enterprises. Crowd-based entrepreneurial business models have encouraged E3 factors in entrepreneurship embedding people's engagement, empowerment of local entrepreneurs including gender sensitivity, and entrepreneurial performance with experience (learn and acquired skills). Contextualizing socio-psychological and anthropological drivers in designing, developing, and delivering entrepreneurial business models within competitive market ecosystems will help in accelerating the entrepreneurial transformation process to converge with contemporary innovation and technology trends.

The entrepreneurial functions confined to niche market limit the proximity of entrepreneurial innovation in competitive markets, which results adversely in changing entrepreneurial desire and foster consumption of entrepreneurial products. The technology and new business models make the proximity proposition of local enterprises easier to move between consumers, alliance partners, and social institutions to improve the intertwining of consumption with low-cost innovation and marketing process. The game analytics in unmasking the challenges in transitional entrepreneurship is largely based on the problems, needs, and solutions (PNS) factors explored through consumer interactions. In addition, crowd influence towards ideation, design thinking, crowd funding, and brand-elevated marketing play major role in transforming entrepreneurial practices. R3 analytics comprising the social and entrepreneurial resilience to changing entrepreneurship style influences divergent factors of returns and risks associated with transitional and transformational entrepreneurship patterns. Based on these game analytics, entrepreneurs must develop a transformational game map, which needs to be supported through public programs and socio-political leadership

Large industries in various sectors such as consumer electronics are developing consortiums of micro, small, and medium-sized enterprises to serve as original equipment manufacturers (OEM) and supply components for manufacturing. Large industries commonly serve as value added resellers (VAR) for both industrial and consumer goods. Consequently, most OEMs operate in an umbrella of respective mother companies. The product design, manufacturing process, quality control, marketing strategy, and value creation activities are supported by the mother companies, which operate as VAR. These companies stay abreast the consortium enterprises of contemporary fashion trends and operate with the contemporary business model. Nonetheless, the social media and collective intelligence help the OEMs and the mother company to learn about the shifts in consumer preference, market trends, and the changing PNS factor (problems, needs, and expected solutions) of consumers and stakeholders. Manufacturing at the micro, small, and medium enterprises has gradually transformed over the years by reducing the marketing responsibilities and to serve as a feeder channel for the mother companies. Consequently, these firms have laid more emphasis on improving their core competencies to serve as feeder channel for mother companies or contracting firms. The trend of channelizing micro, small, and medium industries to serve as feeder sources for mother companies in a consortium system has built the reputation as reliable manufacturers. Many of these firms have entered the market successfully with their niche brands alongside operating directly with the contracting firms (Wang et al., 2014).

The process of transforming conventional entrepreneurship should begin with adequate knowledge on the perspectives of PNS factors comprising embedded problems, needs, and solutions within the society in the context of cost-benefit-profit and cost-time-risk factors associated with innovation and technology. To meet the social challenges at the grassroots, entrepreneurs adapt to frugal innovations, while large companies tend to explore opportunities to commercialize innovation that have been developed and experimented successfully at the bottom of the pyramid entrepreneurial segment. The reverse innovation process can be explained as connecting global markets with innovation at the niche level. The low-cost technology is preferred by the entrepreneurs at the niche level to develop high value utilitarian products and attract large industries to explore opportunities to commercialize the innovation lying at the bottom-of-the-pyramid. Consequently, large companies are engaged in transfer of technology to small enterprises and develop entrepreneurial consortiums by industry and by region to improve their quality and performance of the product. Such streamlining of entrepreneurial products between upstream and downstream markets facilitates quick movement of products and services at macro level. However, micro and small enterprises are critical at adapting to low-cost technology and long technology lifecycle in manufacturing products (Molina & Rajagopal, 2023). The rapidly changing enterprise management system provides agility in entrepreneurial transitions by restructuring organizational design, operational efficiency, and strategy development. The increasing opportunities of technology-oriented enterprises and shifts in the operational patterns have triggered upstream growth in the global market, which needs to be meticulously handled in transformational enterprises within the scope of their resources. The strategic implications of PESTEL factors (political, economic, social, technological, environmental, and legal) on management of these enterprises are critical to the transformation process of conventional enterprises as micro, small, and medium enterprises largely depend on social and public programs for holistic support.

Future Perspectives

Innovation of new products is a complex process that needs to be carried out meticulously in the firms integrating the business and consumer use values in the marketplace. Firms engaged in innovating products should map consumers' needs, attributes of close substitutes, competitive threats, required product services, and estimated cost of marketing of the product in different markets. However, the rate of failure of innovative services is higher as compared to the consumer products. Limited creativity, low capital resources, and access to technology widely affect the low-cost customer-centric innovation in competitive markets. Fragmentation of entrepreneurial infrastructure and resources affects the quality of entrepreneurial production by narrowing down the proximity to market. Consequently, the diffusion of innovations of micro, small, and medium enterprises is encapsulated within the low economic segments of consumers limiting the knowledge of entrepreneurial brands and the competitive markets. The creative innovations of entrepreneurs should be enabled with disruptive potential to override commercial brands in competitive markets. The effective use of social networks should be encouraged among entrepreneurs for the diffusion of innovation and disseminating customer value. The community entrepreneurship centers such as craft development centers of India may be organized in developing countries to provide training on technology and managerial know-how in managing cost-effective process of innovative products development and overcome the resource crisis.

Most companies consider the process of innovative product development as colossal due to the cumbersome stage gate process of manufacturing, and organizational and market-led intricacies in analyzing key indicators to launch and manage the products in the competitive marketplace. However, the process of developing an innovative product can be made easier by rationally dividing the chronology of process into two parts—an early stage that focuses on evaluating prospects and eliminating bad bets, and a late stage that optimizes the market potential (Rajagopal, 2021). Ideation process for new product development can be stimulated through metaphors, pictures, and experience. It is rooted in the philosophy of rationalism and empiricism, implying 'the truth is out there' approaches. It is observed that defining cognitive idea generation is based on personal experiences and beliefs driven by individual and social information. However, these forms of cognitive-based idea generation process are individualistic and not amenable to team contexts (Bhatt, 2000). There is typically an indirect connection between investment in research, innovation, and commercial benefit. Research is more likely to help generating ideas through the available information and public resources. More significantly, as discoveries are likely to be in the form of laws of nature, abstract ideas, and physical phenomena, they are likely to be converged with the end user values and market potential from the perspective of business firms (Abernathy & Utterback, 1978). Besides technology and machine learning, creativity among entrepreneurs can be encouraged with focus on PNS factors by simplifying innovation concept and the utilitarian promise to create high perceived value. Frugal innovations should focus on major consumer benefits to enable the entrepreneurial brands to differentiate the competing products and enhance the user experience and product outreach.

Co-creating blueprints, infrastructure layouts, and building cognitive cosmos, the innovation project charter led to develop customer-centric and social business models. Most companies in the competitive marketplace shift ideas to gain competitive leverage and tend to seed, synergize, and serve the market target. The most important lesson for entrepreneurs and leaders to learn in the innovation process is how to think about innovation and nurture it in the interest of the firm and market (Hargadon & Sutton, 2001). Innovative emphasis shifts from product function to process development and refinement. Process-focused innovations in this stage are likely to be radical rather than incremental. Besides Fintech projects, entrepreneurs today leverage investor networks to attract donations or equity-based crowdfunding through designing campaigns on social media channels. Customer value in terms of satisfaction, use value, retailing practices, price, quality, and media appreciation is one of the indicators for building brand value for the non-conventional products and unfamiliar brands of a firm. Customer value concepts may be applied by the firms to evaluate the product performance of an innovative product in the given market and determine the approach for gaining competitive advantage over the traditional products. For gaining long-term returns on the aggregate customer value, firms may need to methodically estimate the profitability associated thereof in terms of product attractiveness, volume of buying, and market share while introducing the new products in a competitive market environment (Rajagopal, 2021).

Growth and acceleration in restructuring the accountable gender entrepreneurship (GARAGE), an inclusive business-linked entrepreneurial model, can be promoted through social and government programs to create value for low-income communities through social or profit-based business projects that integrate the business activities into the value chain of a company. The inclusive businesses build strategic relationship with the stakeholders and key partners, and engage them in business planning, strategy development, implementation, and performance evaluation in a sustainable way. Inclusive businesses face challenging circumstances in low-income markets, which may influence the configuration of the business model in context of the socio-economic attributes of the ecosystem at the bottom-of-the-pyramid. However, the lack of formal market institutions in low-income markets causes uncertain demand, high transaction costs, low purchasing power, and cannibalization by the local brands. Consequently, firm aiming to work with inclusive businesses to serve the customers at bottom-of-the-pyramid needs to look at the alternative ways to lower the transaction costs and empower stakeholders in marketing process (Rajagopal, 2022). Such inclusive development of women entrepreneurs will be consistent with the GARAGE change agent model as discussed in the pre-text. The transition of conventional enterprises to the contemporary ecosystem is marked by a discrete path within the known, less known, and unknown space as exhibited in Fig. 5.2.

Entrepreneurial transition has a complex trajectory across the spaces of acquaintance. Entrepreneurs identify conventional wisdom, leadership of family business, and the status of entrepreneurial resources as the prominent features of the known space. Their experience in entrepreneurial productivity and managing revenue stream indicates the complexity of market due to changing preferences of consumers and penetration of disruptive innovations. In addition, the short lifecycle of technologies restricts the creativity and economic performance of the enterprise. Broadly, the less known space as illustrated in Fig. 5.2 indicates the entrepreneurial access to high cost and complex technology in using artificial intelligence (AI), machine learning (ML), augmented reality (AR), virtual reality (VR), and large language models (LLM). Consequently, most micro, small, and medium enterprises are unable to adapt to hybrid or digital entrepreneurship. In addition, the robotic intervention in manufacturing, packaging, and processing under industry 4.0 and 5.0 revolution appears to be a far cry among micro, small, and medium enterprises. The bridge between known and less known spaces that could stimulate entrepreneurial transition to a higher level is determined by real-time tracking, value-based innovation, and affordable technology. The awareness about the elements of less known space is significantly contributed through collective intelligence and digital networks.

The continuous research and development, corporate investment, and high risk-taking ability of large firms in experimentation and commercialization at the enterprise level in unknown space have emerged as a big challenge. The technology companies engaged in developing cyber parks to host technology-led enterprises with long technology lifecycle and low entrepreneurial risk have shown promising development. The growing use of metaverse and 4D printing by entwining neural networks are exploring the unknown entrepreneurial transition space. Promoting the uphill entrepreneurial journey through such transitions requires entrepreneurial education and skill development, change proneness among entrepreneurs and transition management through 4As (awareness, attributes, affordability, and adaptability) and 4Cs comprising cost-to-entrepreneurs (tangible and intangible), convenience (workspace), communication (guidelines), and conflict resolution (quick solutions).

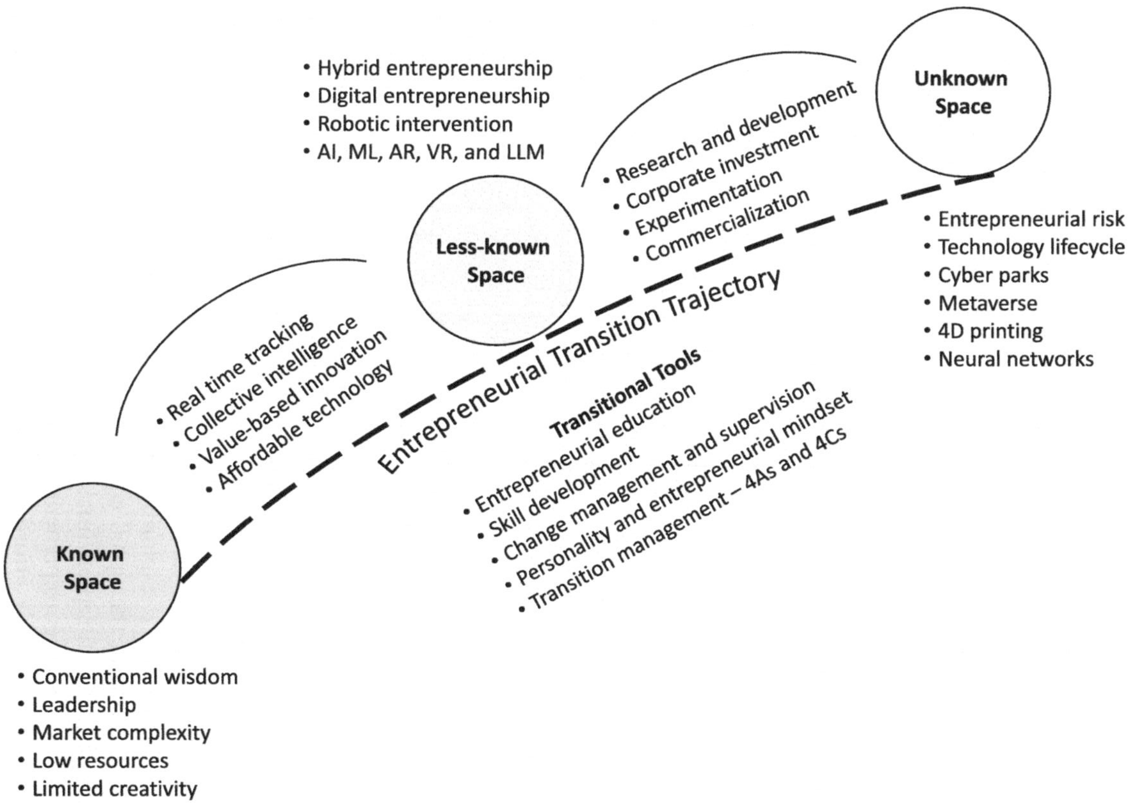

Fig. 5.2 Pathway of entrepreneurial transition (*Source* Authors)

Unilever's social strategy of empowering rural women through the Shakti program (Shakti meaning Power in Hindi language) to create brand awareness and community marketing, and support economic well-being at the household level in India has created enormous customer value and sustainable behavior. Project Shakti enables rural women in villages across India in inculcating an entrepreneurial mindset and helps them become financially independent marketers of Hindustan Unilever Limited (HUL) products. To provide them regular income, these women entrepreneurs are trained on the basic principles of distribution management and familiarization with the company's products. In this process, rural sales promoters coach women by familiarizing them with HUL products to manage their businesses better. Imparting such training in women entrepreneurs develops soft skills of negotiation and communication and prepares them as business associates of the company. This strategy of empowering rural women to expand the market horizon of HUL is consistent with the elements of the design cube. Shakti project was a win-win initiative taken by HUL to conquer the universe of market (premium, upper mass, economic mass, lower mass, and bottom-of-the-pyramid). The bottom-of-the market was aimed to be covered through the Shakti project. The broad task of the project was to promote sales and distribution of HUL products through several embedded initiatives. The Shakti initiative of HUL is a perfect blend of performance with purpose by creating social values, corporate values, and market values simultaneously. This experiment was a good fit to the design cube concept as it explains all the three facets of the cube comprising design-to-market, design-to-society, and design-to-value (Rajagopal, 2022). Inclusive business in developing countries is growing increasingly profitable by operating on digital platforms, which has encouraged firms to co-create mainstream innovations. These companies are based on the collective intelligence and socially conscious learning that has significantly pushed the inclusive venturing capabilities. Such firms are being leveraged to explore inclusive business strategically and invest more systematically within the ecosystem business models. Inclusive businesses are maturing in the farm- and non-farm sector businesses with the growing support of public policies, and supply chain and payments infrastructure. These firms as emerging companies purpose-built to serve design engaging people at the bottom-of-the-pyramid (Wernick & Upadhyay, 2021).

The business ecosystem today has observed a radical shift due to manifold growth of information and communication technology and extensive digitization of business processes. Such radical shift in businesses has been induced by the increased use of Internet to stimulate the ambidextrous digitization at the corporate and stakeholder levels. The dependency on Web-based technologies has brought disruptive changes to the spatial landscape of business through the creation of an entire host of digital marketing tactics, customer convenience, and competitiveness. Managers need to prioritize the development of preferred business models; they wish to work with and determine which technology to adopt in marketing practices to gain both strategic and tactical leverage. The business competition has a complex grid of prospectors, analyzers, low-cost defenders, and differentiated defenders. Prospector firms gain the first mover advantage of new products or services and initially play tactics to leapfrog competitors' offerings develop. These firms attempt to lead the market and stay differentiated among the challenger and follower firms in the marketplace. It is the process by which behavioral changes occur as a cognitive appraisal of experience on usefulness of technology. In the interactive learning process, emotions affect the customer value and influence the intention to adapt to technological innovations (Kim et al., 2016). Mobile technology applications have stimulated consumers in evaluating the competing offerings, using interactive technology to reaffirm buying decisions and making purchases, and engaging with on-site client services to resolve any product or delivery conflicts. Transformation of retailing services such as 360° product views and features, informational touch points, interactive displays, and applications for mobile devices has increased the perceived usefulness of these technology attributes among consumers (Grewal et al., 2017).

Continuous innovation and technology in the consumer products companies have set new trends in the market and created dynamic value perceptions among consumers that have raised their preferences and expectations. Digital marketing has opened massive opportunities to deliver new consumer experiences and strengthened the relationships with consumers across the destinations in the global marketplace. Digital disruption has created new dimensions in consumer marketing through the benefits of large-scale promotions and convenience to drive compulsive buying behavior among consumers. The platform economy has shown a huge shift in the creation of consumer value. However, technology- and born-digital businesses have led the innovations, which is being experienced by consumers in every sector now. The platform economy distinctly comprises a new set of business and economic relations that depend on the Internet, computation, and data. The ecosystem created by each platform is a source of value, and it sets the terms, by which users can participate. Such business and economic platform has empowered consumers and developed their bargaining potential for quality and value for money (Rajagopal, 2020).

Most of the innovations triggered by the start-up enterprises are woven around the needs and preferences of consumer towards convenience, sustainable technology, and value for money bargain. Such product innovations include technology-driven products for the mass consumers. Gaining access to and deploying these innovations easily and cost-effectively in the market drives the success of companies today. The new technology trends in twenty-first century affect the innovation process of consumer-centric and business-to-business oriented start-up enterprises. These enterprises need to develop radical differentiation in innovative products to make them sensitive to the top-of-the-mind and gain competitive advantage. A blend of technology and taste of consumers will enrich low-cost high-value products and build brand acquaintance among consumers in various geo-demographic segments including urban settlements. An engineer by training, who spent months perfecting the recipe for coconut chips, which he needed for his mother's Thai lettuce wraps, worked on innovative coconut chips with five flavors from Salted Caramel to Original. He developed a family business to export his innovative snacks from Thailand. In 2014, his products won 'The Best Snack Award' in Fancy Foods show, USA, and in 2012, the entrepreneur built a non-GMO certified company known as Dang Foods in Berkley, CA, with the exclusivity of his innovation. Such business projects originate from the start-ups and evolve to a larger scale, provided the innovations are nurtured properly during the business evolution process (Rajagopal, 2022).

References

Abernathy, W. J., & Utterback, J. M. (1978). Patterns of innovation in industry. *Technology Review, 80*(7), 40–47.

Ahl, H., & Marlow, S. (2012). Exploring the dynamics of gender, feminism, and entrepreneurship: Advancing debate to escape a dead end? *Organization, 19*(5), 543–562.

Battilana, J., & Lee, M. (2014). Advancing research on hybrid organizing–insights from the study of social enterprises. *Academy of Management Annals, 8*, 397–441.

Bhatt, G. (2000). Organising knowledge in the knowledge development cycle. *Journal of Knowledge Management, 4*(1), 15–26.

Brugmann, J., & Prahalad, C. K. (2007). Cocreating business's new social compact. *Harvard Business Review, 85*(2), 80–90.

Czubala, M. R., Puente, M., & Corullon, C. (2022). Rural depopulation in Spain: Next generation EU as a stimulus to accelerate the transformation. *Journal of Liberty and International Affairs, 8*(1), 211–228.

Fontana, R. (2007). Technical change, prices and communications technology: Insights from the local area networking industry. *Technological Forecasting and Social Change, 74*(3), 313–330.

Galindo, M. A., & Méndez-Picazo, M.-T. (2013). Innovation, entrepreneurship and economic growth. *Management Decision, 51*(3), 501–514.

Grewal, D., Roggeveen, A. L., & Nordfält, J. (2017). The future of retailing. *Journal of Retailing, 93*(1), 1–6.

Gupta, M., & Dharwal, M. (2022). Green entrepreneurship and sustainable development: A conceptual framework. *Materials Today: Proceedings, 49*(8), 3603–3606.

Hargadon, A., & Sutton, R. I. (2001). Building an innovation factory. *Harvard Business Review, 78*(3), 157–166.

Harsanto, B., Mulyana, A., Faisal, Y. A., & Shandy, V. M. (2022). Open innovation for sustainability in the social enterprises: An empirical evidence. *Journal of Open Innovation: Technology, Market, and Complexity, 8*(3), 160. https://doi.org/10.3390/joitmc8030160

Kim, H. Y., Lee, J. Y., Mun, J. M., & Johnson, K. K. (2016). Consumer adoption of smart in-store technology: Assessing the predictive value of attitude versus beliefs in the technology acceptance model. *International Journal of Fashion Design, Technology and Education, 10*(1), 26–36.

Molina, A., & Rajagopal. (2023). *Challenge-based learning, research, and innovation: Leveraging industry, government, and society*. Springer.

Rajagopal. (2020). *Market entropy: How to manage chaos and uncertainty for improving organizational performance*. Business Expert Press.

Rajagopal. (2021). *Crowd-based business models—Using collective intelligence for market competitiveness*. Palgrave Macmillan.

Rajagopal. (2022). *Evolving with inclusive business in emerging markets: Managing the new bottom-line*. Business Expert Press.

Rajagopal. (2023). *Proximity marketing: Converging community, consciousness, and consumption*. Business Expert Press.

Ratten, V., & Jones, P. (2021). Entrepreneurship and management education: Exploring trends and gaps. *International Journal of Management in*

Education, 19(1), Article 100431. https://doi.org/10.1016/j.ijme.2020.10043

Vodă, A., & Florea, N. (2019). Impact of personality traits and entrepreneurship education on entrepreneurial intentions of business and engineering students. *Sustainability, 11*(4), 1–34.

Wang, Y., Niu, B., & Guo, P. (2014). The comparison of two vertical outsourcing structures under push and pull contracts. *Production and Operations Management, 23*(4), 610–625.

Wellalage, N. H., & Fernandez, V. (2019). Innovation and SME finance: Evidence from developing countries. *International Review of Financial Analysis, 66*, 1–14.

Wernick, D. A., & Upadhyay, S. K. (2021). Does the U.S. hospitality market offer fertile soil for Lemon Tree Hotels' inclusive business model? *Harvard Business School Press*.

Index

Rajagopal and A. Rajagopal, *Unmasking Invisible Challenges in Entrepreneurship*, Palgrave Studies of Entrepreneurship and Social Challenges in Developing Economies,
https://doi.org/10.1007/978-3-031-63653-0

SPRINGER NATURE

GPSR Compliance

The European Union's (EU) General Product Safety Regulation (GPSR) is a set of rules that requires consumer products to be safe and our obligations to ensure this.

If you have any concerns about our products, you can contact us on ProductSafety@springernature.com

In case Publisher is established outside the EU, the EU authorized representative is:

Springer Nature Customer Service Center GmbH
Europaplatz 3
69115 Heidelberg, Germany

The manufacturer's authorised representative in the EU is Springer
Nature Customer Service Centre GmbH, Europaplatz 3, 69115 Heidelberg,
Germany. If you have any concerns regarding our products, please
contact ProductSafety@springernature.com

Printed and bound by CPI Group (UK) Ltd, Croydon, CR0 4YY
01/10/2026
02225978-0016